영어 원서로 읽는 셜록 2

*The Sign of Four*

**영어 원서로 읽는 셜록 2 - The Sign of Four**
Reading Sherlock without a Dictionary 2 - The Sign of Four (Korean Edition)
Sir Arthur Conan Doyle

펴낸곳: 북스트릿
주소: 서울시 은평구 연서로 17길 28-10 302호
지은이: 아서 코난 도일 Arthur Conan Doyle
일러스트레이터: 리하르트 거트슈미트 Richard Gutschmidt
편집 및 주석: 신찬범
북커버 및 내지 디자인: 북스트릿
E-mail: invino70@gmail.com
Homepage: https://bookstreetpress.modoo.at
Blog: blog.naver.com/invino70
Fax: 0504-405-6711
초판 1쇄 2019년 12월 9일
초판 2쇄 2021년 02월 27일

© 2019 북스트릿 BookStreet
북스트릿의 허락없는 이 책의 일부 또는 전부의 무단 복제, 전재, 발췌를 금합니다

ISBN: 979-11-965278-9-1

영어 원서로 읽는 셜록 2
The Sign of Four

Sir Arthur Conan Doyle

북스트릿
BookStreet

# 머리말

이 책은 영문 고전을 깊이 있게 이해하고 감상하기 위해 기획되었습니다.

영어 원서를 읽는 데에 있어서 가장 큰 어려움 중 하나는 생소한 단어와 구 등을 매번 영어사전에서 찾아봐야 하는 번거로움입니다. 이러한 이유로 영어 원서의 독해가 쉽지 않은 것으로 인식되고 있으며, 특히 영어가 모국어가 아닌 분이나 영어를 공부하시는 분에게 어려움이 있습니다.

이 책은 이러한 어려움을 고려하여 영어 원서를 읽는 도중에 빈번하게 영어사전을 찾아봐야 하는 번거로움을 대폭 줄였으며, 영어사전을 될 수 있는 대로 적게 참조하면서 더 수월하게 영어 원서를 읽을 수 있게 했습니다.

이 책에는 영문 고전의 원본 텍스트가 수록되어 있습니다. 문장 해석에 중요한 숙어, 구동사, 그 외 어려운 단어와 구 들을 선택하고 강조했습니다. 이들 단어와 구를 각 페이지 왼쪽에 단락별로 정의하고 설명했습니다. 각 단어의 발음기호를 기재하여, 어휘력을 높이는 데 도움이 되게 했습니다. 또한, 스토리 흐름을 이해하기 위한 시놉시스를 책 말미에 추가했습니다.

이 책이 독자분이 영문 고전을 읽는 데 의미 있는 도움이 되기를 바랍니다.

신찬범

# The Sign of Four

1 The Science of Deduction ········································ 11

2 The Statement of the Case ······································ 24

3 In Quest of a Solution ············································ 33

4 The Story of the Bald-Headed Man ······················ 41

5 The Tragedy of Pondicherry Lodge ······················ 56

6 Sherlock Holmes Gives a Demonstration ············ 68

7 The Episode of the Barrel ······································ 82

8 The Baker Street Irregulars ·········· 100

9 A Break in the Chain ·········· 115

10 The End of the Islander ·········· 130

11 The Great Agra Treasure ·········· 144

12 The Strange Story of Jonathan Small ·········· 154

네 사람의 서명 시놉시스 ·········· 192

# The Sign of Four

# 1 *The Science of Deduction*

mantelpiece [mæntlpìːs] n.
벽난로 선반
hypodermic [hàipədə́ːrmik] adj.
피하 주사의
sinewy [sínjuːi] adj.
건장한

Sherlock Holmes took his bottle from the corner of the **mantel-piece** and his **hypodermic** syringe from its neat morocco case. With his long, white, nervous fingers he adjusted the delicate needle, and rolled back his left shirt-cuff. For some little time his eyes rested thoughtfully upon the **sinewy** forearm and wrist all dotted and scarred with innumerable puncture-marks. Finally he thrust the sharp point home, pressed down the tiny piston, and sank back into the velvet-lined arm-chair with a long sigh of satisfaction.

on the contrary: 반대로

Three times a day for many months I had witnessed this performance, but custom had not reconciled my mind to it. **On the contrary**, from day to day I had become more irritable at the sight,

conscience [kánʃəns / kɔ́n-] n.
양심, 도덕심
nonchalant [nɑ̀nʃ-əlá:nt, nɑ́nʃ-
ələnt / nɔ́n-] adj.
냉담한, 무관심한
liberty [líbə:rti] n.
도를 넘은 자유, 멋대로의 행동
diffident [dífidənt] adj.
조심스러운, 수줍은
cross [krɔ:s / krɔs] v.
to interfere with, 간섭하다, 반대하다

Beaune [boun] n.
부르고뉴 산 레드와인
exasperation [igzæ̀spəréiʃən] n.
격노, 분개
hold out: 지속하다, 견디다

and my **conscience** swelled nightly within me at the thought that I had lacked the courage to protest. Again and again I had registered a vow that I should deliver my soul upon the subject, but there was that in the cool, **nonchalant** air of my companion which made him the last man with whom one would care to take anything approaching to a **liberty**. His great powers, his masterly manner, and the experience which I had had of his many extraordinary qualities, all made me **diffident** and backward in **crossing** him.

Yet upon that afternoon, whether it was the **Beaune** which I had taken with my lunch, or the additional **exasperation** produced by the extreme deliberation of his manner, I suddenly felt that I could **hold out** no longer.

# 1 The Science of Deduction    13

"Which is it to-day?" I asked,—"morphine or cocaine?"

He raised his eyes **languidly** from the old black-letter volume which he had opened.

"It is cocaine," he said,—"a seven-per-cent. solution. Would you care to try it?"

"No, indeed," I answered, **brusquely**. "My **constitution** has not **got over** the Afghan **campaign** yet. I cannot afford to throw any extra strain upon it."

He smiled at my **vehemence**. "Perhaps you are right, Watson," he said. "I suppose that its influence is physically a bad one. I find it, however, so **transcendently** stimulating and clarifying to the mind that its secondary action is a matter of small **moment**."

"But consider!" I said, earnestly. "Count the cost! Your brain may, as you say, be roused and excited, but it is a **pathological** and **morbid** process, which involves increased tissue-change and may at last leave a permanent weakness. You know, too, what a black reaction comes upon you. Surely the game is hardly **worth the candle**. Why should you, for a mere passing pleasure, risk the loss of those great powers with which you have been **endowed**? Remember that I speak not only as one comrade to another, but as a medical man to one for whose constitution he is to some extent **answerable**."

He did not seem offended. On the contrary, he put his finger-tips together and leaned his elbows on the arms of his chair, like one who has a **relish** for conversation.

---

languidly[lǽŋgwidli] adv.
맥없이, 나른하게

brusquely [brʌskli / bruskli] adv.
무뚝뚝하게, 퉁명스럽게
constitution [kɑ̀nstətjúːʃən / kɔ̀n-] n.
체격, 체질
get over:
극복하다, 이겨내다
campaign [kæmpéin] n.
전투
vehemence [víːəməns] n.
열정, 열의, 격렬함
transcendently [trænséndəntli] adv. 뛰어나게, 초월적으로
moment [móumənt] n.
중요성, 긴요함
pathological [pæ̀θəládʒikəl / -lɔ́dʒ-] adj.
병리학의, 병적인
morbid [mɔ́ːrbid] adj.
병적인, 병에 걸린
not worth the candle:
보람없는, 가치없는
endow [endáu] v.
주다, 부여하다
answerable [ǽnsərəbl, ɑ́ːn-] adj.
책임이 있는, 상관이 있는

relish [réliʃ] n.
음미, 애호

stagnation [stægneiʃən] n.
침체, 부진
abstruse [æbstrúːs] adj.
난해한, 이해하기 어려운
cryptogram [kríptougræ̀m] n.
암호
intricate [íntrəkit] adj.
뒤엉킨, 복잡한
dispense with:
~없이 지내다
abhor [æbhɔ́ːr] v.
질색하다, 싫어하다
crave [kreiv] v.
간절히 원하다, 열망하다

"... But I abhor the dull routine of existence. I crave for mental exaltation..."

cordially [kɔ́ːrdʒəli / -diəli] adv.
성심껏, 진심으로

exact science:
정밀과학 (물리, 화학, 천문학 등)
tinge [tindʒ] v.
느낌을 주다, 기미를 풍기게 하다

"My mind," he said, "rebels at **stagnation**. Give me problems, give me work, give me the most **abstruse cryptogram** or the most **intricate** analysis, and I am in my own proper atmosphere. I can **dispense** then **with** artificial stimulants. But I **abhor** the dull routine of existence. I **crave** for mental exaltation. That is why I have chosen my own particular profession,—or rather created it, for I am the only one in the world."

"The only unofficial detective?" I said, raising my eyebrows.

"The only unofficial consulting detective," he answered. "I am the last and highest court of appeal in detection. When Gregson or Lestrade or Athelney Jones are out of their depths—which, by the way, is their normal state—the matter is laid before me. I examine the data, as an expert, and pronounce a specialist's opinion. I claim no credit in such cases. My name figures in no newspaper. The work itself, the pleasure of finding a field for my peculiar powers, is my highest reward. But you have yourself had some experience of my methods of work in the Jefferson Hope case."

"Yes, indeed," said I, **cordially**. "I was never so struck by anything in my life. I even embodied it in a small brochure with the somewhat fantastic title of 'A Study in Scarlet.'"

He shook his head sadly.

"I glanced over it," said he. "Honestly, I cannot congratulate you upon it. Detection is, or ought to be, an **exact science**, and should be treated in the same cold and unemotional manner. You have attempted to **tinge** it with romanticism, which

| | |
|---|---|
| elopement [ilóup-] n.<br>(결혼 등을 위해) 남녀가 함께 달아남 | |
| remonstrate [rimánstreit, rémənstrèit / rimɔ́nstreit] v.<br>항의하다, 불만을 말하다 | |
| tamper [tǽmpəːr] v.<br>함부로 변경하다, 손을 대다 | |
| unravel [ʌnrǽvəl] v.<br>풀다, 해결하다 | |
| didactic [daidǽktik] adj.<br>교훈적인, 설교적인 | |
| the Continent:<br>(영국을 제외한) 유럽, 대륙 | |
| intuition [intjuíʃən] n.<br>직관 | |
| deficient [difíʃənt] adj.<br>부족한, 모자란 | |

produces much the same effect as if you worked a love-story or an **elopement** into the fifth proposition of Euclid."

"But the romance was there," I **remonstrated**. "I could not **tamper** with the facts."

"Some facts should be suppressed, or at least a just sense of proportion should be observed in treating them. The only point in the case which deserved mention was the curious analytical reasoning from effects to causes by which I succeeded in **unraveling** it."

I was annoyed at this criticism of a work which had been specially designed to please him. I confess, too, that I was irritated by the egotism which seemed to demand that every line of my pamphlet should be devoted to his own special doings. More than once during the years that I had lived with him in Baker Street I had observed that a small vanity underlay my companion's quiet and **didactic** manner. I made no remark, however, but sat nursing my wounded leg. I had had a Jezail bullet through it some time before, and, though it did not prevent me from walking, it ached wearily at every change of the weather.

"My practice has extended recently to **the Continent**," said Holmes, after a while, filling up his old brier-root pipe. "I was consulted last week by François Le Villard, who, as you probably know, has come rather to the front lately in the French detective service. He has all the Celtic power of quick **intuition**, but he is **deficient** in the wide range of exact knowledge which is essential to the higher developments of his art. The case was

profusion [prəfjúːʒən] n.
풍부함
magnifique:
(French) 훌륭한, 위대한
coup de maîtres:
(French) 대가의 솜씨
tour de force:
(French) 수완, 놀라운 재주l
ardent:[áːrdənt] adj.
열렬한, 정열적인

deduction [didʌ́kʃən] n.
추론, 추리, 연역
wanting [wɔ́(ː)ntiŋ, wánt-] adj.
부족한, 결여된
in time: sooner or later, 장차, 조만간

guilty [gílti] adj.
유죄의, 가책받는, 꺼림칙한
monograph [mánəgræf, -gràːf / mɔ́n-] n.
학술논문
enumerate [injúːmərèit] v.
열거하다, 나열하다, 하나하나 세다
supreme [səpríːm, su(ː)-] adj.
가장 중요한, 궁극의

concerned with a will, and possessed some features of interest. I was able to refer him to two parallel cases, the one at Riga in 1857, and the other at St. Louis in 1871, which have suggested to him the true solution. Here is the letter which I had this morning acknowledging my assistance." He tossed over, as he spoke, a crumpled sheet of foreign notepaper. I glanced my eyes down it, catching a **profusion** of notes of admiration, with stray "*magnifiques*," "*coup-de-maîtres*," and "*tours-de-force*," all testifying to the **ardent** admiration of the Frenchman.

"He speaks as a pupil to his master," said I.

"Oh, he rates my assistance too highly," said Sherlock Holmes, lightly.

"He has considerable gifts himself. He possesses two out of the three qualities necessary for the ideal detective. He has the power of observation and that of **deduction**. He is only **wanting** in knowledge; and that may come **in time**. He is now translating my small works into French."

"Your works?"

"Oh, didn't you know?" he cried, laughing. "Yes, I have been **guilty** of several **monographs**. They are all upon technical subjects. Here, for example, is one 'Upon the Distinction between the Ashes of the Various Tobaccos.' In it I **enumerate** a hundred and forty forms of cigar-, cigarette-, and pipe-tobacco, with colored plates illustrating the difference in the ash. It is a point which is continually turning up in criminal trials, and which is sometimes of **supreme** importance as a clue. If you can say definitely, for example, that some

# 1 The Science of Deduction

narrow [nǽrou, -rə] v.
좁게 하다, 좁히다, 제한하다

minutiae [minjuːʃiː] n.
사소한 것, 상세

compositor [kəmpázətir / -pɔ́z-] n.
식자공, 조판공

antecedent [æntəsíːdənt] n.
전력, 경력, 내력

wreath [riːθ] n.
동그라미, 소용돌이

murder had been done by a man who was smoking an Indian lunkah, it obviously **narrows** your field of search. To the trained eye there is as much difference between the black ash of a Trichinopoly and the white fluff of bird's-eye as there is between a cabbage and a potato."

"You have an extraordinary genius for **minutiae**," I remarked.

"I appreciate their importance. Here is my monograph upon the tracing of footsteps, with some remarks upon the uses of plaster of Paris as a preserver of impresses. Here, too, is a curious little work upon the influence of a trade upon the form of the hand, with lithotypes of the hands of slaters, sailors, corkcutters, **compositors**, weavers, and diamond-polishers. That is a matter of great practical interest to the scientific detective,—especially in cases of unclaimed bodies, or in discovering the **antecedents** of criminals. But I weary you with my hobby."

"Not at all," I answered, earnestly. "It is of the greatest interest to me, especially since I have had the opportunity of observing your practical application of it. But you spoke just now of observation and deduction. Surely the one to some extent implies the other."

"Why, hardly," he answered, leaning back luxuriously in his arm-chair, and sending up thick blue **wreaths** from his pipe. "For example, observation shows me that you have been to the Wigmore Street Post-Office this morning, but deduction lets me know that when there you dispatched a telegram."

"Right!" said I. "Right on both points! But I

impulse [ímpʌls] n.
충동, 일시적인 감정

chuckle [tʃʌ́kl] v.
소리없이 웃다
superfluous [su:pə́:rfluəs] adj.
과잉의, 여분의
mold, mould [mould] n.
흙
instep [ínstèp] n.
발등

"For example, observation shows me that you have been to the Wigmore Street Post-Office this morning, but deduction lets me know that when there you dispatched a telegram."

impertinent [impə́:rtənənt] adj.
무례한, 주제넘은

on the contrary:
반대로

confess that I don't see how you arrived at it. It was a sudden **impulse** upon my part, and I have mentioned it to no one."

"It is simplicity itself," he remarked, **chuckling** at my surprise,—"so absurdly simple that an explanation is **superfluous**; and yet it may serve to define the limits of observation and of deduction. Observation tells me that you have a little reddish **mould** adhering to your **instep**. Just opposite the Wigmore Street Office they have taken up the pavement and thrown up some earth which lies in such a way that it is difficult to avoid treading in it in entering. The earth is of this peculiar reddish tint which is found, as far as I know, nowhere else in the neighborhood. So much is observation. The rest is deduction."

"How, then, did you deduce the telegram?"

"Why, of course I knew that you had not written a letter, since I sat opposite to you all morning. I see also in your open desk there that you have a sheet of stamps and a thick bundle of post-cards. What could you go into the post-office for, then, but to send a wire? Eliminate all other factors, and the one which remains must be the truth."

"In this case it certainly is so," I replied, after a little thought.

"The thing, however, is, as you say, of the simplest. Would you think me **impertinent** if I were to put your theories to a more severe test?"

"**On the contrary**," he answered, "it would prevent me from taking a second dose of cocaine. I should be delighted to look into any problem which you might submit to me."

# 1 The Science of Deduction

"I have heard you say that it is difficult for a man to have any object in daily use without leaving the impress of his individuality upon it in such a way that a trained observer might read it. Now, I have here a watch which has recently come into my possession. Would you have the kindness to let me have an opinion upon the character or habits of the late owner?"

I handed him over the watch with some slight feeling of amusement in my heart, for the test was, as I thought, an impossible one, and I intended it as a lesson against the somewhat **dogmatic** tone which he occasionally assumed. He balanced the watch in his hand, gazed hard at the dial, opened the back, and examined the works, first with his naked eyes and then with a powerful **convex lens**.

dogmatic [dɔ(:)gmǽtik, dɑg-] adj.
독단적인, 독선적인
convex lens:
볼록렌즈
cf. concave lens

"... Eliminate all other factors, and the one which remains must be the truth."

crestfallen[ˈfɔ́:lən] adj.
의기소침한

lame [leim] adj.
불충분한, 설득력 없는
impotent [ímpətənt] adj.
무력한, 허약한

barren [bǽrən] adj.
쓸데없는, 헛된
lackluster [lǽklʌ̀stəːr] adj.
흐리멍덩한
subject to ~:
~을 조건으로, ~을 전제로 하여
inherit [inhérit] v.
물려받다, 상속하다
gather [gǽðər] v.
추측하다

untidy [ʌntáidi] adj.
단정치 못한, 흐트러진

I could hardly keep from smiling at his **crestfallen** face when he finally snapped the case to and handed it back.

"There are hardly any data," he remarked. "The watch has been recently cleaned, which robs me of my most suggestive facts."

"You are right," I answered. "It was cleaned before being sent to me."

In my heart I accused my companion of putting forward a most **lame** and **impotent** excuse to cover his failure. What data could he expect from an uncleaned watch?

"Though unsatisfactory, my research has not been entirely **barren**," he observed, staring up at the ceiling with dreamy, **lack-lustre** eyes. "**Subject to** your correction, I should judge that the watch belonged to your elder brother, who **inherited** it from your father."

"That you **gather**, no doubt, from the H. W. upon the back?"

"Quite so. The W. suggests your own name. The date of the watch is nearly fifty years back, and the initials are as old as the watch: so it was made for the last generation. Jewelry usually descends to the eldest son, and he is most likely to have the same name as the father. Your father has, if I remember right, been dead many years. It has, therefore, been in the hands of your eldest brother."

"Right, so far," said I. "Anything else?"

"He was a man of **untidy** habits,—very untidy and careless. He was left with good prospects, but he threw away his chances, lived for some time in poverty with occasional short intervals of

take to: 습관이 되다, 좋아하게 되다

limp [limp] v.
다리를 절다
bitterness [bítərnis] n.
쓴맛, 괴로움, 쓰라림, 반감
unworthy [ʌnwə́:rði] adj.
품위에 어울리지 않는, 천박한, 야비한
descend [disénd] v.
타락하다, 비굴하게 행동하다
charlatanism [ʃɑ́:rlətənìzəm] n.
야바위, 엉터리

pray [prei] v.
please, "I pray you"의 생략형, 바라건대, 아무쪼록

follow [fálou / fɔ́lou] v.
이해하다

1 The Science of Deduction　　21

prosperity, and finally, **taking to** drink, he died. That is all I can gather."

I sprang from my chair and **limped** impatiently about the room with considerable **bitterness** in my heart.

"This is **unworthy** of you, Holmes," I said. "I could not have believed that you would have **descended** to this. You have made inquires into the history of my unhappy brother, and you now pretend to deduce this knowledge in some fanciful way. You cannot expect me to believe that you have read all this from his old watch! It is unkind, and, to speak plainly, has a touch of **charlatanism** in it."

"My dear doctor," said he, kindly, "**pray** accept my apologies. Viewing the matter as an abstract problem, I had forgotten how personal and painful a thing it might be to you. I assure you, however, that I never even knew that you had a brother until you handed me the watch."

"Then how in the name of all that is wonderful did you get these facts? They are absolutely correct in every particular."

"Ah, that is good luck. I could only say what was the balance of probability. I did not at all expect to be so accurate."

"But it was not mere guess-work?"

"No, no: I never guess. It is a shocking habit,—destructive to the logical faculty. What seems strange to you is only so because you do not **follow** my train of thought or observe the small facts upon which large inferences may depend. For example, I began by stating that your brother was careless. When you observe the lower part of that watch-case

dint [dint] v.
움푹 들어가게 하다
feat [fi:t] n.
묘기, 뛰어난 재주
cavalierly [kæ̀vəlíərli] adv.
되는대로, 무심하게
farfetched [fɑːr̀fétʃt] adj.
무리한, 억지의, 당치않은
inference [ínfərəns] n.
추론, 추리
inherit [inhérit] v.
물려받다, 상속하다

pawnbroker [pɔ́ːbròukər] n.
전당포주인
transpose [trænspóuz] v.
뒤바꾸다
redeem [ridíːm] v.
갚다, 상환하다, (저당 등을) 도로 찾다, 되찾다
pledge [pledʒ] n.
저당, 담보
sober [sóubəːr] adj.
술 취하지 않은, 맑은 정신의
drunkard [drʌ́ŋkərd] n.
술고래
unsteady [ʌnstédi] adj.
불안정한, 흔들리는

on foot: 진행 중인

you notice that it is not only **dinted** in two places, but it is cut and marked all over from the habit of keeping other hard objects, such as coins or keys, in the same pocket. Surely it is no great **feat** to assume that a man who treats a fifty-guinea watch so **cavalierly** must be a careless man. Neither is it a very **far-fetched inference** that a man who **inherits** one article of such value is pretty well provided for in other respects."

I nodded, to show that I followed his reasoning.

"It is very customary for **pawnbrokers** in England, when they take a watch, to scratch the number of the ticket with a pin-point upon the inside of the case. It is more handy than a label, as there is no risk of the number being lost or **transposed**. There are no less than four such numbers visible to my lens on the inside of this case. Inference,—that your brother was often at low water. Secondary inference,—that he had occasional bursts of prosperity, or he could not have **redeemed** the **pledge**. Finally, I ask you to look at the inner plate, which contains the key-hole. Look at the thousands of scratches all round the hole,—marks where the key has slipped. What **sober** man's key could have scored those grooves? But you will never see a **drunkard**'s watch without them. He winds it at night, and he leaves these traces of his **unsteady** hand. Where is the mystery in all this?"

"It is as clear as daylight," I answered. "I regret the injustice which I did you. I should have had more faith in your marvellous faculty. May I ask whether you have any professional inquiry **on**

**foot** at present?"

"None. Hence the cocaine. I cannot live without brain-work. What else is there to live for? Stand at the window here. Was ever such a **dreary**, **dismal**, **unprofitable** world? See how the yellow fog **swirls** down the street and drifts across the dun-colored houses. What could be more hopelessly **prosaic** and **material**? What is the use of having powers, doctor, when one has no field upon which to exert them? Crime is commonplace, existence is commonplace, and no qualities **save** those which are commonplace have any function upon earth."

I had opened my mouth to reply to this **tirade**, when with a crisp knock our landlady entered, bearing a card upon the brass **salver**.

"A young lady for you, sir," she said, addressing my companion.

"Miss Mary Morstan," he read. "Hum! I have no recollection of the name. Ask the young lady to step up, Mrs. Hudson. Don't go, doctor. I should prefer that you remain."

---

dreary [dríəri] adj.
우울한, 황량한
dismal [dízməl] adj.
음울한, 쓸쓸한
unprofitable [ʌnpráfitəbəl / -próf-] adj.
무익한, 헛된
swirl [swə:rl] v.
소용돌이치다
prosaic [prouzéiik] adj.
흥미없는, 지루한
material [mətí-əriəl] adj.
물질적인, 세속적인
save [seiv] prep.
except, ~을 제외하고
tirade [táireid, tiréid] n.
장황한 열변
salver [sǽlvə:r] n.
쟁반

"... Was ever such a dreary, dismal, unprofitable world? See how the yellow fog swirls down the street and drifts across the dun-colored houses. What could be more hopelessly prosaic and material? ..."

# 2 *The Statement of the Case*

composure [kəmpóuʒər] n.
침착, 평정
dainty [déinti] adj.
우아한, 고상한
somber [sámbər / sɔ́m-] adj.
어두운, 어두컴컴한
amiable [éimiəbəl] adj.
상냥한, 호의적인

Miss Morstan entered the room with a firm step and an outward **composure** of manner. She was a blonde young lady, small, **dainty**, well gloved, and dressed in the most perfect taste. There was, however, a plainness and simplicity about her costume which bore with it a suggestion of limited means. The dress was a **sombre** grayish beige, untrimmed and unbraided, and she wore a small turban of the same dull hue, relieved only by a suspicion of white feather in the side. Her face had neither regularity of feature nor beauty of complexion, but her expression was sweet and **amiable**, and her large blue eyes were singularly spiritual and sympathetic. In an experience of women which extends over many nations and three

quiver [kwívər] v.
떨리다
agitation [æ̀dʒətéiʃən] n.
동요, 불안

unravel [ʌnrǽvəl] v.
풀다, 해결하다

utterly [ʌ́tərli] adv.
아주, 완전히
inexplicable [inéksplikəbəl, ìniksplík-] adj.
설명할 수 없는, 해석할 수 없는
glisten [glísn] v.
반짝반짝 빛나다

brisk [brisk] adj.
활발한, 기운찬

detain [ditéin] v.
붙들다, 구류하다
inestimable [inéstəməbəl] adj.
헤아릴 수 없는
relapse [rilǽps] v.
되돌아가다

## 2 The Statement of the Case

separate continents, I have never looked upon a face which gave a clearer promise of a refined and sensitive nature. I could not but observe that as she took the seat which Sherlock Holmes placed for her, her lip trembled, her hand **quivered**, and she showed every sign of intense inward **agitation**.

"I have come to you, Mr. Holmes," she said, "because you once enabled my employer, Mrs. Cecil Forrester, to **unravel** a little domestic complication. She was much impressed by your kindness and skill."

"Mrs. Cecil Forrester," he repeated thoughtfully. "I believe that I was of some slight service to her. The case, however, as I remember it, was a very simple one."

"She did not think so. But at least you cannot say the same of mine. I can hardly imagine anything more strange, more **utterly inexplicable**, than the situation in which I find myself."

Holmes rubbed his hands, and his eyes **glistened**. He leaned forward in his chair with an expression of extraordinary concentration upon his clear-cut, hawklike features.

"State your case," said he, in **brisk**, business tones.

I felt that my position was an embarrassing one.

"You will, I am sure, excuse me," I said, rising from my chair.

To my surprise, the young lady held up her gloved hand to **detain** me.

"If your friend," she said, "would be good enough to stop, he might be of **inestimable** service to me."

I **relapsed** into my chair.

regiment [rédʒəmənt] n.
연대 聯隊
relative [rélətiv] n.
친척, 친족, 인척
leave [li:v] n.
휴가, 허가
direct [dirékt, dai-] v.
지시하다, 명령하다, 시키다
at once:
곧, 즉시, 당장에

"Briefly," she continued, "the facts are these. My father was an officer in an Indian **regiment** who sent me home when I was quite a child. My mother was dead, and I had no **relative** in England. I was placed, however, in a comfortable boarding establishment at Edinburgh, and there I remained until I was seventeen years of age. In the year 1878 my father, who was senior captain of his regiment, obtained twelve months' **leave** and came home. He telegraphed to me from London that he had arrived all safe, and **directed** me to come down **at once**, giving the Langham Hotel as his address. His message, as I remember, was full of kindness and love. On reaching London I drove to the Langham, and was informed that Captain Morstan was staying there, but that he had gone

Our inquiries led to no result; and from that day to this no word has ever been heard of my unfortunate father.

out the night before and had not yet returned. I waited all day without news of him. That night, on the advice of the manager of the hotel, I communicated with the police, and next morning we advertised in all the papers. Our inquiries led to no result; and from that day to this no word has ever been heard of my unfortunate father. He came home with his heart full of hope, to find some peace, some comfort, and instead—"

She put her hand to her throat, and a **choking** sob cut short the sentence.

"The date?" asked Holmes, opening his note-book.

"He disappeared upon the 3rd of December, 1878,—nearly ten years ago."

"His luggage?"

"Remained at the hotel. There was nothing in it to suggest a clue,—some clothes, some books, and a considerable number of **curiosities** from **the Andaman Islands**. He had been one of the officers in charge of the convict-guard there."

"Had he any friends in town?"

"Only one that we know of,—Major Sholto, of his own regiment, the 34th Bombay Infantry. The major had retired some little time before, and lived at Upper Norwood. We communicated with him, of course, but he did not even know that his brother officer was in England."

"A **singular** case," remarked Holmes.

"I have not yet described to you the most singular part. About six years ago—to be exact, upon the 4th of May, 1882—an advertisement appeared in *The Times* asking for the address of Miss Mary Morstan and stating that it would be to her advantage to come forward. There was no name or address **appended**. I had at that time just entered the family of Mrs. Cecil Forrester in the capacity of **governess**. By her advice I published my address in the advertisement column. The same day there arrived through the post a small card-board box addressed to me, which I found to contain a very large and **lustrous** pearl. No word of writing was enclosed. Since then every year upon the same date there has always appeared a similar box, containing a similar pearl, without any clue as to the sender. They have been pronounced by an expert to be of a rare variety and of considerable value. You can see for yourselves that they are very **handsome**."

She opened a flat box as she spoke, and showed me six of the finest pearls that I had ever seen.

"Your statement is most interesting," said Sherlock Holmes. "Has anything else occurred to you?"

"Yes, and no later than to-day. That is why I have come to you. This morning I received this letter, which you will perhaps read for yourself."

"Thank you," said Holmes. "The envelope too, please. Postmark, London, S.W. Date, July 7. Hum! Man's thumb-mark on corner,—probably postman. Best quality paper. Envelopes at sixpence a packet. Particular man in his stationery. No address. 'Be at the third pillar from the left outside the Lyceum Theatre to-night at seven o'clock. If you are **distrustful**, bring two friends. You are a wronged woman, and shall have justice. Do not bring police. If you do, all will be **in vain**. Your unknown friend.' Well, really, this is a very pretty little mystery. What do you intend to do, Miss Morstan?"

"That is exactly what I want to ask you."

"Then we shall most certainly go. You and I and—yes, why, Dr. Watson is the very man. Your **correspondent** says two friends. He and I have worked together before."

"But would he come?" she asked, with something appealing in her voice and expression.

"I should be proud and happy," said I, **fervently**, "if I can be of any service."

"You are both very kind," she answered. "I have led a **retired** life, and have no friends whom I could appeal to. If I am here at six it will do, I suppose?"

"You must not be later," said Holmes. "There is one other point, however. Is this handwriting the same as that upon the pearl-box addresses?"

"I have them here," she answered, producing half a dozen pieces of paper.

"You are certainly a **model client**. You have the correct **intuition**. Let us see, now." He spread out the papers upon the table, and gave little darting glances from one to the other. "They are disguised hands, except the letter," he said, presently, "but there can be no question **as to** the authorship. See how the irrepressible Greek e will break out, and see the **twirl** of the final s. They are undoubtedly by the same person. I should not like to suggest false hopes, Miss Morstan, but is there any resemblance between this hand and that of your father?"

"Nothing could be more unlike."

"I expected to hear you say so. We shall look

pray [prei] v.
please, "I pray you"의 생략형,
바라건대, 아무쪼록
au revoir [òurəvwá:r]
(French) 작별 인사 farewell,
see you again

briskly [briskli] adv.
활발히, 기운차게
speck [spek] n.
반점, 얼룩
somber [sámbər / sóm-] adj.
어두컴컴한

languidly [læŋgwidli] adv.
맥없이, 나른하게
automaton [ɔ:támətàn / ɔ:túmətən] n.
자동 인형, 로봇
inhuman [inhjú:mən] adj.
비인간적인, 냉혹한, 몰인정한
bias [báiəs] v.
편견을 갖게 하다
antagonistic [æntægənístik] adj.
상극의
winning [wíniŋ] adj.
매력적인
repellent [ripélənt] adj.
불쾌한, 기분 나쁜
acquaintance [əkwéintəns] n.
아는 사람, 친분관계, 일면식
philanthropist [filǽnərəpist] n.
박애주의자
disprove [disprú:v] v.
반증하다, 논박하다

out for you, then, at six. **Pray** allow me to keep the papers. I may look into the matter before then. It is only half-past three. *Au revoir*, then."

"*Au revoir*," said our visitor, and, with a bright, kindly glance from one to the other of us, she replaced her pearl-box in her bosom and hurried away.

Standing at the window, I watched her walking **briskly** down the street, until the gray turban and white feather were but a **speck** in the **sombre** crowd.

"What a very attractive woman!" I exclaimed, turning to my companion.

He had lit his pipe again, and was leaning back with drooping eyelids.

"Is she?" he said, **languidly**. "I did not observe."

"You really are an **automaton**,—a calculating-machine!" I cried. "There is something positively **inhuman** in you at times."

He smiled gently.

"It is of the first importance," he said, "not to allow your judgment to be **biased** by personal qualities. A client is to me a mere unit,—a factor in a problem. The emotional qualities are **antagonistic** to clear reasoning. I assure you that the most **winning** woman I ever knew was hanged for poisoning three little children for their insurance-money, and the most **repellent** man of my **acquaintance** is a **philanthropist** who has spent nearly a quarter of a million upon the London poor."

"In this case, however—"

"I never make exceptions. An exception **disproves** the rule. Have you ever had occasion to

# 2 The Statement of the Case

study character in handwriting? What do you make of this fellow's **scribble**?"

"It is **legible** and regular," I answered. "A man of business habits and some force of character."

Holmes shook his head.

"Look at his long letters," he said. "They hardly rise above the common herd. That d might be an a, and that l an e. Men of character always **differentiate** their long letters, however **illegibly** they may write. There is **vacillation** in his k's and **self-esteem** in his capitals. I am going out now. I have some few references to make. Let me recommend this book,—one of the most remarkable ever penned. It is Winwood Reade's *Martyrdom of Man*. I shall be back in an hour."

I sat in the window with the volume in my hand, but my thoughts were far from the daring speculations of the writer. My mind ran upon our late visitor,—her smiles, the deep rich tones of her voice, the strange mystery which overhung her life. If she were seventeen at the time of her father's disappearance she must be seven-and-twenty now,—a sweet age, when youth has lost its self-consciousness and become a little sobered by experience. So I sat and mused, until such dangerous thoughts came into my head that I hurried away to my desk and **plunged** furiously into the latest **treatise** upon **pathology**. What was I, an army surgeon with a weak leg and a weaker banking-account, that I should dare to think of such things? She was a unit, a factor,—nothing more. If my future were black, it was better surely to

---

scribble [skríb-əl] n.
필적, 낙서, 휘갈겨 쓴 것
legible [lédʒəb-əl] adj.
읽을 수 있는, 판독할 수 있는

differentiate [dìfərénʃièit] v.
분간하다, 구별하다
illegibly [ilédʒəbəli] adv.
읽기 어렵게, 판독하기 어렵게
vacillation [væsəléiʃən] n.
동요, 주저, 흔들림
self-esteem [sélfestíːm] n.
자존심, 자부심

plunge [plʌndʒ] v.
뛰어들다, 몰두하다
treatise [tríːtis, -tiz] n.
논문, 전문서적
pathology [pəθúlədʒi / -ɔ́l-] n.
병리학

"You really are an automaton,—a calculating-machine!" I cried. "There is something positively inhuman in you at times."

will o' the wisps [wíləðəwísp] n. 도깨비불, 환영

face it like a man than to attempt to brighten it by mere **will-o'-the-wisps** of the imagination.

If my future were black, it was better surely to face it like a man than to attempt to brighten it by mere will-o'-the-wisps of the imagination.

# 3 In Quest of a Solution

fit [fit] n.
일시적 격발, 일시적 기분

It was half-past five before Holmes returned. He was bright, eager, and in excellent spirits,—a mood which in his case alternated with **fits** of the blackest depression.

"There is no great mystery in this matter," he said, taking the cup of tea which I had poured out for him. "The facts appear to admit of only one explanation."

"What! you have solved it already?"

suggestive [səgdʒéstiv] adj.
시사하는, 암시하는

"Well, that would be too much to say. I have discovered a **suggestive** fact, that is all. It is, however, *very* suggestive. The details are still to be added. I have just found, on consulting the back files of *The Times*, that Major Sholto, of Upper Norword, late of the 34th Bombay Infantry, died upon the 28th of April, 1882."

obtuse [əbtjúːs] adj.
둔감한, 이해가 느린

"I may be very **obtuse**, Holmes, but I fail to see

what this suggests."

"No? You surprise me. Look at it in this way, then. Captain Morstan disappears. The only person in London whom he could have visited is Major Sholto. Major Sholto denies having heard that he was in London. Four years later Sholto dies. *Within a week of his death* Captain Morstan's daughter receives a valuable present, which is repeated from year to year, and now **culminates** in a letter which describes her as a wronged woman. What wrong can it refer to except this **deprivation** of her father? And why should the presents begin immediately after Sholto's death, unless it is that Sholto's **heir** knows something of the mystery and desires to make compensation? Have you any alternative theory which will meet the facts?"

"But what a strange compensation! And how strangely made! Why, too, should he write a letter now, rather than six years ago? Again, the letter speaks of giving her justice. What justice can she have? It is too much to suppose that her father is still alive. There is no other injustice in her case that you know of."

"There are difficulties; there are certainly difficulties," said Sherlock Holmes, **pensively**. "But our **expedition** of to-night will solve them all. Ah, here is a four-wheeler, and Miss Morstan is inside. Are you all ready? Then we had better go down, for it is a little past the hour."

I picked up my hat and my heaviest stick, but I observed that Holmes took his revolver from his drawer and slipped it into his pocket. It was clear that he thought that our night's work might

---

culminate [kʌ́lmənèit] v.
정점을 이루다, 마침내 ~이 되다
deprivation [dèprəvéiʃən] n.
상실, 손실, 박탈
heir [ɛər] n.
상속인, 계승자

pensively [pénsivli] adv.
심각하게, 숙고하여
expedition [èkspədíʃən] n.
(집단, 단체의) 모험, 원정

## 3 In Quest of a Solution

be a serious one.

Miss Morstan was muffled in a dark **cloak**, and her sensitive face was **composed**, but pale. She must have been more than woman if she did not feel some uneasiness at the strange enterprise upon which we were **embarking**, yet her self-control was perfect, and she readily answered the few additional questions which Sherlock Holmes put to her.

"Major Sholto was a very particular friend of papa's," she said. "His letters were full of allusions to the major. He and papa were in command of the troops at the Andaman Islands, so they were thrown a great deal together. By the way, a curious paper was found in papa's desk which no one could understand. I don't suppose that it is of the slightest importance, but I thought you might care to see it, so I brought it with me. It is here."

Holmes unfolded the paper carefully and smoothed it out upon his knee. He then very methodically examined it all over with his double lens.

"It is paper of native Indian manufacture," he remarked. "It has at some time been pinned to a board. The **diagram** upon it appears to be a plan of part of a large building with numerous halls, corridors, and passages. At one point is a small cross done in red ink, and above it is '3.37 from left,' in faded pencil-writing. In the left-hand corner is a curious **hieroglyphic** like four crosses in a line with their arms touching. Beside it is written, in very rough and coarse characters, 'The sign of the four,—Jonathan Small, Mahomet Singh, Abdullah Khan, Dost Akbar.' No, I confess that I

---

cloak [klouk] n.
망토, 외투
composed [kəmpóuzd] adj.
침착한, 조용한, 차분한
embark [embá:rk, im-] v.
착수하다, 시작하다

diagram [dáiəgræ̀m] n.
그림, 약도
hieroglyphic [hàiərəglífik] n.
상형문자

bear upon:
관계되다, 관련이 있다

Beside it is written, in very rough and coarse characters, 'The sign of the four,—Jonathan Small, Mahomet Singh, Abdullah Khan, Dost Akbar.'

undertone [ʌ́ndərtòun] n.
낮은 목소리
impenetrable [impénətrəbəl] adj. 꿰뚫을 수 없는, 들어갈 수 없는
reserve [rizə́:rv] n.
냉담함, 신중함, 침묵

dreary [dríəri] adj.
우울한, 황량한
drizzly [drízli] adj.
이슬비의, 이슬비와 같은
splotch [splatʃ / splɔtʃ] n.
반점, 얼룩
slimy [sláimi] adj.
질척한, 끈적끈적한
murky [mə́:rki] adj.
어둑한
thoroughfare [θə́:roufɛ̀ə:r] n.
도로
eerie [íəri] adj.
으스스한, 무시무시한
flit [flit] v.
경쾌하게 움직이다
haggard [hǽgərd] adj.
수척한, 초췌한

do not see how this **bears upon** the matter. Yet it is evidently a document of importance. It has been kept carefully in a pocket-book; for the one side is as clean as the other."

"It was in his pocket-book that we found it."

"Preserve it carefully, then, Miss Morstan, for it may prove to be of use to us. I begin to suspect that this matter may turn out to be much deeper and more subtle than I at first supposed. I must reconsider my ideas."

He leaned back in the cab, and I could see by his drawn brow and his vacant eye that he was thinking intently. Miss Morstan and I chatted in an **undertone** about our present expedition and its possible outcome, but our companion maintained his **impenetrable reserve** until the end of our journey.

It was a September evening, and not yet seven o'clock, but the day had been a **dreary** one, and a dense **drizzly** fog lay low upon the great city. Mud-colored clouds drooped sadly over the muddy streets. Down the Strand the lamps were but misty **splotches** of diffused light which threw a feeble circular glimmer upon the **slimy** pavement. The yellow glare from the shop-windows streamed out into the steamy, vaporous air, and threw a **murky**, shifting radiance across the crowded **thoroughfare**. There was, to my mind, something **eerie** and ghost-like in the endless procession of faces which **flitted** across these narrow bars of light,—sad faces and glad, **haggard** and merry. Like all human kind, they flitted from the gloom into the light, and so back into

petty [péti] adj.
사소한, 하찮은, 이차적인
jot [dʒɑt / dʒɔt] v.
간결하게 적다, 간단히 메모하다

hansom [hǽnsəm] n.
핸섬형 2륜마차
rattle [rǽtl] v.
덜걱대다
brisk [brisk] adj.
활발한, 기운찬
accost [əkɔ́(:)st, əkást] v.
접근하다, 말 걸다

dogged [dɔ́(:)gid, dág-] adj.
완고한, 끈질긴, 고집 센

street Arab:
부랑아, 방랑자, 정처 없는 사람

the gloom once more. I am not subject to impressions, but the dull, heavy evening, with the strange business upon which we were engaged, combined to make me nervous and depressed. I could see from Miss Morstan's manner that she was suffering from the same feeling. Holmes alone could rise superior to **petty** influences. He held his open note-book upon his knee, and from time to time he **jotted** down figures and memoranda in the light of his pocket-lantern.

At the Lyceum Theatre the crowds were already thick at the side-entrances. In front a continuous stream of **hansoms** and four-wheelers were **rattling** up, discharging their cargoes of shirt-fronted men and beshawled, bediamonded women. We had hardly reached the third pillar, which was our rendezvous, before a small, dark, **brisk** man in the dress of a coachman **accosted** us.

"Are you the parties who come with Miss Morstan?" he asked.

"I am Miss Morstan, and these two gentlemen are my friends," said she.

He bent a pair of wonderfully penetrating and questioning eyes upon us.

"You will excuse me, miss," he said with a certain **dogged** manner, "but I was to ask you to give me your word that neither of your companions is a police-officer."

"I give you my word on that," she answered.

He gave a shrill whistle, on which a **street Arab** led across a four-wheeler and opened the door. The man who had addressed us mounted to the box, while we took our places inside. We had

errand [érənd] n.
용건, 볼일
hoax [houks] n.
속임수, 날조
inconceivable [ìnkənsí:vəbəl] adj. 상상도 할 수 없는, 믿을 수 없는
hypothesis [haipáθəsis / -pɔ́θ-] n. 가설
demeanor [dimí:nər] n. 품행, 태도
resolute [rézəlù:t] adj. 의지가 굳은, 단호한
collected [kəléktid] adj. 침착한, 태연한
reminiscences [rèmənís-əns] n. 회고, 회상
anecdote [ǽnikdòut] n. 재미있는 사건, 일화 逸話, 비사 秘史

We had hardly done so before the driver whipped up his horse, and we plunged away at a furious pace through the foggy streets.

hardly done so before the driver whipped up his horse, and we plunged away at a furious pace through the foggy streets.

The situation was a curious one. We were driving to an unknown place, on an unknown **errand**. Yet our invitation was either a complete **hoax**,— which was an **inconceivable hypothesis**,—or else we had good reason to think that important issues might hang upon our journey. Miss Morstan's **demeanor** was as **resolute** and **collected** as ever. I endeavored to cheer and amuse her by **reminiscences** of my adventures in Afghanistan; but, to tell the truth, I was myself so excited at our situation and so curious as to our destination that my stories were slightly involved. To this day she declares that I told her one moving **anecdote** as to how a musket looked into my tent at the dead

of night, and how I fired a double-barrelled tiger cub at it. At first I had some idea as to the direction in which we were driving; but soon, what with our pace, the fog, and my own limited knowledge of London, I lost my bearings, and knew nothing, **save** that we seemed to be going a very long way. Sherlock Holmes was never at fault, however, and he **muttered** the names as the cab rattled through squares and in and out by **tortuous** by-streets.

"Rochester Row," said he. "Now Vincent Square. Now we come out on the Vauxhall Bridge Road. We are making for the Surrey side, apparently. Yes, I thought so. Now we are on the bridge. You can catch **glimpses** of the river."

We did indeed get a fleeting view of a stretch of the Thames with the lamps shining upon the broad, silent water; but our cab dashed on, and was soon involved in a **labyrinth** of streets upon the other side.

"Wordsworth Road," said my companion. "Priory Road. Lark Hall Lane. Stockwell Place. Robert Street. Cold Harbor Lane. Our quest does not appear to take us to very fashionable regions."

We had, indeed, reached a **questionable** and **forbidding** neighborhood. Long lines of dull brick houses were only relieved by the coarse glare and **tawdry** brilliancy of **public houses** at the corner. Then came rows of two-storied villas each with a fronting of miniature garden, and then again **interminable** lines of new, staring brick buildings,—the monster **tentacles** which the giant city was throwing out into the country. At last the cab

---

save [seiv] prep.
except, ~을 제외하고
mutter [mʌ́tər] v.
낮게 중얼거리다
tortuous [tɔ́:rtʃuəs] adj.
구불구불한

glimpse [glimps] n.
언뜻 눈에 띄임

labyrinth [lǽbərìnθ] n.
미로

questionable [kwéstʃənəbəl] adj.
의심스러운, 불확실한
forbidding [fəːrbídiŋ] adj.
험악한, 위태로운
tawdry [tɔ́:dri] adj.
화려하고 값싼
public house:
선술집
interminable intə́:rmənəbəl] adj.
끝없는, 계속되는
tentacle [téntək-əl] n.
촉수, 촉각

hindoo [híndu:] adj.
힌두교의
clad [klæd] v.
(古·詩) clothe의 과거, 과거분사
sash [sæʃ] n.
장식띠
incongruous [inkáŋgruəs /
-kɔ́ŋ-] adj.
어울리지 않는, 조화되지 않는


sahib [sá:hib] n.
(in India) sir; master 인도인이
쓰던 유럽인에 대한 존칭
khidmutgar, khitmutgar [kíd-
mətgà:r] n.
(Indian) 급사

drew up at the third house in a new terrace. None of the other houses were inhabited, and that at which we stopped was as dark as its neighbors, save for a single glimmer in the kitchen window. On our knocking, however, the door was instantly thrown open by a **Hindoo** servant **clad** in a yellow turban, white loose-fitting clothes, and a yellow **sash**. There was something strangely **incongruous** in this Oriental figure framed in the commonplace door-way of a third-rate suburban dwelling-house.

"The **Sahib** awaits you," said he, and even as he spoke there came a high piping voice from some inner room.

"Show them in to me, ***khitmutgar***," it cried. "Show them straight in to me."

# 4 *The Story of the Bald-Headed Man*

sordid [sɔ́:rdid] adj.
더러운, 누추한
scalp [skælp] n.
두피, 머리피부
writhe [raið] v.
몸을 뒤틀다, 몸부림치다
scowl [skaul] v.
얼굴을 찡그리다, 인상을 찌푸리다
repose [ripóuz] n.
평온, 평정
pendulous [péndʒələs] adj.
늘어진, 매달린
irregular [irégjələr] adj.
불규칙한, 가지런하지 않은

We followed the Indian down a **sordid** and common passage, ill lit and worse furnished, until he came to a door upon the right, which he threw open. A blaze of yellow light streamed out upon us, and in the centre of the glare there stood a small man with a very high head, a bristle of red hair all round the fringe of it, and a bald, shining **scalp** which shot out from among it like a mountain-peak from fir-trees. He **writhed** his hands together as he stood, and his features were in a perpetual jerk, now smiling, now **scowling**, but never for an instant in **repose**. Nature had given him a **pendulous** lip, and a too visible line of yellow and **irregular** teeth, which he strove feebly to conceal by constantly passing his hand over the

in spite of: ~에도 불구하고
obtrusive [əbtrú:siv] adj. 두드러진, 돌출한

sanctum [sǽŋktəm] n. 신성한 장소
howling [háuliŋ] adj. 황량한, 쓸쓸한

athwart [əθwɔ́:rt] adv. 가로질러, 횡단하여
hookah [húkə] n. 물담배

stethoscope [stéθəskòup] n. 청진기

lower part of his face. **In spite of** his **obtrusive** baldness, he gave the impression of youth. In point of fact he had just turned his thirtieth year.

"Your servant, Miss Morstan," he kept repeating, in a thin, high voice.

"Your servant, gentlemen. Pray step into my little **sanctum**. A small place, miss, but furnished to my own liking. An oasis of art in the **howling** desert of South London."

We were all astonished by the appearance of the apartment into which he invited us. In that sorry house it looked as out of place as a diamond of the first water in a setting of brass. The richest and glossiest of curtains and tapestries draped the walls, looped back here and there to expose some richly-mounted painting or Oriental vase. The carpet was of amber-and-black, so soft and so thick that the foot sank pleasantly into it, as into a bed of moss. Two great tiger-skins thrown **athwart** it increased the suggestion of Eastern luxury, as did a huge **hookah** which stood upon a mat in the corner. A lamp in the fashion of a silver dove was hung from an almost invisible golden wire in the centre of the room. As it burned it filled the air with a subtle and aromatic odor.

"Mr. Thaddeus Sholto," said the little man, still jerking and smiling.

"That is my name. You are Miss Morstan, of course. And these gentlemen—"

"This is Mr. Sherlock Holmes, and this is Dr. Watson."

"A doctor, eh?" cried he, much excited. "Have you your **stethoscope**? Might I ask you—would you

mitral [máitrəl] adj.
승모판의

have the kindness? I have grave doubts as to my **mitral** valve, if you would be so very good. The aortic I may rely upon, but I should value your opinion upon the mitral."

I listened to his heart, as requested, but was unable to find anything **amiss**, **save** indeed that he was in an ecstasy of fear, for he shivered from head to foot.

amiss [əmís] adj.
잘못된, 정상이 아닌
save [seiv] prep.
except, ~을 제외하고

"It appears to be normal," I said. "You have no cause for uneasiness."

"You will excuse my anxiety, Miss Morstan," he remarked, **airily**. "I am a great sufferer, and I have long had suspicions as to that valve. I am delighted to hear that they are **unwarranted**. **Had your father**, Miss Morstan, **refrained** from throwing a strain upon his heart, he might have been alive now."

airily [ɛ́ərəli] adv.
경쾌하게, 쾌활하게
unwarranted [ʌnwɔ́(:)rəntid, -wɑ́r-] adj.
근거없는, 정당화되지 않는
Had your father:
If your father had
refrain [rifréin] v.
삼가다, 자제하다
callous [kǽləs] adj.
무감각한, 냉담한

I could have struck the man across the face, so hot was I at this **callous** and off-hand reference to so delicate a matter. Miss Morstan sat down, and her face grew white to the lips.

"I knew in my heart that he was dead," said she.

"I can give you every information," said he, "and, what is more, I can **do** you **justice**; and I will, too, whatever Brother Bartholomew may say. I am so glad to have your friends here, not only as an escort to you, but also as witnesses to what I am about to do and say. The three of us can show a bold front to Brother Bartholomew. But let us have no outsiders,—no police or officials. We can settle everything satisfactorily among ourselves, without any interference. Nothing would annoy Brother Bartholomew more than any publicity."

do justice to :
정당하게 다루다, 제대로 대하다

settee [setí:] n.
긴 의자

balsamic [bɔ:lsǽmik, bæl-] adj.
방향성의, 향기로운
odor [óudər] n.
냄새, 향기
sedative [sédətiv] n.
진정제

disregard [dìsrigá:rd] v.
무시하다, 경시하다, 등한시하다
take the liberty of:
허락없이 ~하다
discretion [diskréʃən] n.
분별, 신중
retiring [ritái-əriŋ] adj.
삼가는, 소극적인, 수줍은
unaesthetic [ʌ̀nesθétik / -i:s-] adj.
보기에 좋지 않은
materialism [məti-əriəlìzəm] n.
물질 만능주의, 실리주의

    He sat down upon a low **settee** and blinked at us inquiringly with his weak, watery blue eyes.

    "For my part," said Holmes, "whatever you may choose to say will go no further."

    I nodded to show my agreement.

    "That is well! That is well!" said he. "May I offer you a glass of Chianti, Miss Morstan? Or of Tokay? I keep no other wines. Shall I open a flask? No? Well, then, I trust that you have no objection to tobacco-smoke, to the mild **balsamic odor** of the Eastern tobacco. I am a little nervous, and I find my hookah an invaluable **sedative**."

    He applied a taper to the great bowl, and the smoke bubbled merrily through the rose-water. We sat all three in a semicircle, with our heads advanced, and our chins upon our hands, while the strange, jerky little fellow, with his high, shining head, puffed uneasily in the centre.

    "When I first determined to make this communication to you," said he,

    "I might have given you my address, but I feared that you might **disregard** my request and bring unpleasant people with you. I **took the liberty**, therefore, of making an appointment in such a way that my man Williams might be able to see you first. I have complete confidence in his **discretion**, and he had orders, if he were dissatisfied, to proceed no further in the matter. You will excuse these precautions, but I am a man of somewhat **retiring**, and I might even say refined, tastes, and there is nothing more **unaesthetic** than a policeman. I have a natural shrinking from all forms of rough **materialism**. I seldom come in contact with the

patron [péitrən] n.
후원자, 후견인
genuine [dʒénjuin] adj.
진품의, 진짜의
connoisseur [kɑ̀nəsə́:r, -súər / kɔ̀n-] n.
감정가, 감식가
partial [pá:rʃəl] adj.
특히 좋아하는, 편애하는

rough crowd. I live, as you see, with some little atmosphere of elegance around me. I may call myself a **patron** of the arts. It is my weakness. The landscape is a **genuine** Corot, and, though a **connoisseur** might perhaps throw a doubt upon that Salvator Rosa, there cannot be the least question about the Bouguereau. I am **partial** to the modern French school."

"You will excuse me, Mr. Sholto," said Miss Morstan, "but I am here at your request to learn something which you desire to tell me. It is very late, and I should desire the interview to be as short as possible."

"At the best it must take some time," he answered; "for we shall certainly have to go to Norwood and see Brother Bartholomew. We

shall all go and try if we can **get the better of** Brother Bartholomew. He is very angry with me for taking the course which has seemed right to me. I had quite high words with him last night. You cannot imagine what a terrible fellow he is when he is angry."

"If we are to go to Norwood it would perhaps be as well to start at once," I ventured to remark.

He laughed until his ears were quite red.

"That would hardly do," he cried. "I don't know what he would say if I brought you in that sudden way. No, I must prepare you by showing you how we all stand to each other. In the first place, I must tell you that there are several points in the story of which I am myself ignorant. I can only lay the facts before you as far as I know them myself.

"My father was, as you may have guessed, Major John Sholto, once of the Indian army. He retired some eleven years ago, and came to live at Pondicherry Lodge in Upper Norwood. He had prospered in India, and brought back with him a considerable sum of money, a large collection of valuable curiosities, and a staff of native servants. With these advantages he bought himself a house, and lived in great luxury. My twin-brother Bartholomew and I were the only children.

"I very well remember the sensation which was caused by the disappearance of Captain Morstan. We read the details in the papers, and, knowing that he had been a friend of our father's, we discussed the case freely in his presence. He used to join in our **speculations as to** what could have happened. Never for an instant did we suspect that he had the whole secret hidden in his own breast,—that of all men he alone knew the fate of Arthur Morstan.

"We did know, however, that some mystery—some positive danger— **overhung** our father. He was very fearful of going out alone, and he always employed two prize-fighters to act as porters at Pondicherry Lodge. Williams, who drove you to-night, was one of them. He was once light-weight champion of England. Our father would never tell us what it was he feared, but he had a most marked **aversion** to men with wooden legs. On one occasion he actually fired his revolver at a wooden-legged man, who proved to be a harmless tradesman **canvassing** for orders. We had to pay a large sum to **hush** the matter up. My brother and I used to think this a mere **whim** of my father's, but events have since led us to change our opinion.

"Early in 1882 my father received a letter from India which was a great shock to him. He nearly fainted at the breakfast-table when he opened it, and from that day he sickened to his death. What was in the letter we could never discover, but I could see as he held it that it was short and written in a scrawling hand. He had suffered for years from an enlarged spleen, but he now became rapidly worse, and towards the end of April we were informed that he was beyond all hope, and that he wished to make a last communication to us.

"When we entered his room he was propped up with pillows and breathing heavily. He **besought** us to lock the door and to come upon either side of the bed. Then, grasping our hands, he made a

---

overhang [òuvərhǽŋ] v.
임박하다, 위협하다
aversion [əvə́:rʒən / -ʃən] n.
혐오, 반감
canvass [kǽnvəs] v.
간청하다, 부탁하다
hush [hʌʃ] v.
조용하게 하다
whim [hwim] n.
변덕

On one occasion he actually fired his revolver at a wooden-legged man, who proved to be a harmless tradesman canvassing for orders.

beseech [bisí:tʃ] v.
(besought or beseeched) 청하다, 바라다

**besetting** [bisétiŋ] adj.
끊임없이 따라다니는, 쉴 새 없이 엄습하는
**withhold** [wiðhóuld, wiθ-] v.
보류하다, 억누르다
**avarice** [ǽvəris] n.
욕심, 탐욕
**chaplet** [tʃǽplit] n.
구슬 목걸이, 구슬 장식
**Agra**: 인도 북부 도시

Early in 1882 my father received a letter from India which was a great shock to him.

**claim** [kleim] v.
요구하다, 주장하다

remarkable statement to us, in a voice which was broken as much by emotion as by pain. I shall try and give it to you in his own very words.

"'I have only one thing,' he said, 'which weighs upon my mind at this supreme moment. It is my treatment of poor Morstan's orphan. The cursed greed which has been my **besetting** sin through life has **withheld** from her the treasure, half at least of which should have been hers. And yet I have made no use of it myself,—so blind and foolish a thing is **avarice**. The mere feeling of possession has been so dear to me that I could not bear to share it with another. See that **chaplet** dipped with pearls beside the quinine-bottle. Even that I could not bear to part with, although I had got it out with the design of sending it to her. You, my sons, will give her a fair share of the **Agra** treasure. But send her nothing—not even the chaplet—until I am gone. After all, men have been as bad as this and have recovered.

"'I will tell you how Morstan died,' he continued. 'He had suffered for years from a weak heart, but he concealed it from every one. I alone knew it. When in India, he and I, through a remarkable chain of circumstances, came into possession of a considerable treasure. I brought it over to England, and on the night of Morstan's arrival he came straight over here to **claim** his share. He walked over from the station, and was admitted by my faithful Lal Chowdar, who is now dead. Morstan and I had a difference of opinion as to the division of the treasure, and we came to heated words. Morstan had sprung out of his chair in a

paroxysm [pǽrəksìzəm] n.
발작
dusky [dʌ́ski] adj.
어두운

distracted [distrǽktid] adj.
당황한
impulse [ímpʌls] n.
충동, 일시적인 감정
gash [gæʃ] n.
큰 상처
inquiry [inkwáiəri, ⋯-, ínkwəri] n.
조사, 심리

ponder [pándər / pɔ́n-] v.
숙고하다, 곰곰 생각하다
my lips are sealed:
비밀을 지키겠다는 약속

**paroxysm** of anger, when he suddenly pressed his hand to his side, his face turned a **dusky** hue, and he fell backwards, cutting his head against the corner of the treasure-chest. When I stooped over him I found, to my horror, that he was dead.

"'For a long time I sat half **distracted**, wondering what I should do. My first **impulse** was, of course, to call for assistance; but I could not but recognize that there was every chance that I would be accused of his murder. His death at the moment of a quarrel, and the **gash** in his head, would be black against me. Again, an official **inquiry** could not be made without bringing out some facts about the treasure, which I was particularly anxious to keep secret. He had told me that no soul upon earth knew where he had gone. There seemed to be no necessity why any soul ever should know.

"'I was still **pondering** over the matter, when, looking up, I saw my servant, Lal Chowdar, in the doorway. He stole in and bolted the door behind him. "Do not fear, Sahib," he said. "No one need know that you have killed him. Let us hide him away, and who is the wiser?" "I did not kill him," said I. Lal Chowdar shook his head and smiled. "I heard it all, Sahib," said he. "I heard you quarrel, and I heard the blow. But **my lips are sealed**. All are asleep in the house. Let us put him away together." That was enough to decide me. If my own servant could not believe my innocence, how could I hope to make it good before twelve foolish tradesmen in a jury-box? Lal Chowdar and I disposed of the body that night, and within a few days the London papers were full of the mysterious

cling [kliŋ] v.
집착하다, 매달리다
restitution [rèstətjúːʃ-ən] n.
보상, 배상

expression [ikspréʃən] n.
얼굴, 표정
malevolence [məlévələns] n.
악의, 증오

It was a bearded, hairy face, with wild cruel eyes and an expression of concentrated malevolence.

save [seiv] prep.
except, ~을 제외하고
conjure [kándʒər, kʌ́n-] v.
상상하다, 머리 속에 그리다
rifle [ráif-əl] v.
뒤지다, 훔쳐가다

disappearance of Captain Morstan. You will see from what I say that I can hardly be blamed in the matter. My fault lies in the fact that we concealed not only the body, but also the treasure, and that I have **clung** to Morstan's share as well as to my own. I wish you, therefore, to make **restitution**. Put your ears down to my mouth. The treasure is hidden in—'

At this instant a horrible change came over his **expression**; his eyes stared wildly, his jaw dropped, and he yelled, in a voice which I can never forget, 'Keep him out! For Christ's sake keep him out!' We both stared round at the window behind us upon which his gaze was fixed. A face was looking in at us out of the darkness. We could see the whitening of the nose where it was pressed against the glass. It was a bearded, hairy face, with wild cruel eyes and an expression of concentrated **ma-levolence**. My brother and I rushed towards the window, but the man was gone. When we returned to my father his head had dropped and his pulse had ceased to beat.

"We searched the garden that night, but found no sign of the intruder, **save** that just under the window a single footmark was visible in the flower-bed. But for that one trace, we might have thought that our imaginations had **conjured** up that wild, fierce face. We soon, however, had another and a more striking proof that there were secret agencies at work all round us. The window of my father's room was found open in the morning, his cupboards and boxes had been **rifled**, and upon his chest was fixed a torn piece of paper, with the

## 4 The Story of the Bald-Headed Man

words 'The sign of the four' scrawled across it. What the phrase meant, or who our secret visitor may have been, we never knew. As far as we can judge, none of my father's property had been actually stolen, though everything had been turned out. My brother and I naturally associated this peculiar incident with the fear which **haunted** my father during his life; but it is still a complete mystery to us."

The little man stopped to relight his hookah and puffed thoughtfully for a few moments. We had all sat absorbed, listening to his extraordinary narrative. At the short account of her father's death Miss Morstan had turned deadly white, and for a moment I feared that she was about to faint. She **rallied** however, on drinking a glass of water which I quietly poured out for her from a Venetian **carafe** upon the side-table. Sherlock Holmes leaned back in his chair with an abstracted expression and the lids drawn low over his glittering eyes. As I glanced at him I could not but think how on that very day he had complained bitterly of the commonplaceness of life. Here at least was a problem which would **tax** his **sagacity to the utmost**. Mr. Thaddeus Sholto looked from one to the other of us with an obvious pride at the effect which his story had produced, and then continued between the puffs of his overgrown pipe.

"My brother and I," said he, "were, as you may imagine, much excited as to the treasure which my father had spoken of. For weeks and for months we dug and **delved** in every part of the garden, without discovering its **whereabouts**. It was

---

haunt [hɔːnt, hɑːnt] v.
괴롭히다

rally [rǽli] v.
회복하다
carafe [kərǽf, -rɑ́ːf] n.
주전자
tax [tæks] v.
무거운 부담을 지우다, 무리를 강요하다
sagacity [səgǽsəti] n.
현명함
to the utmost:
최대한, 힘껏

The window of my father's room was found open in the morning, his cupboards and boxes had been rifled, and upon his chest was fixed a torn piece of paper, with the words 'The sign of the four' scrawled across it.

delve [delv] v.
철저히 조사하다, (땅 등을) 파다
whereabout [hwɛ́-ərəbàuts] n.
소재, 위치, 거처

maddening [mǽdniŋ] adj.
미치게 하는
averse [əvə́:rs] adj.
몹시 싫어하는
destitute [déstətjù:t] adj.
가난한, 빈한한

**maddening** to think that the hiding-place was on his very lips at the moment that he died. We could judge the splendor of the missing riches by the chaplet which he had taken out. Over this chaplet my brother Bartholomew and I had some little discussion. The pearls were evidently of great value, and he was **averse** to part with them, for, between friends, my brother was himself a little inclined to my father's fault. He thought, too, that if we parted with the chaplet it might give rise to gossip and finally bring us into trouble. It was all that I could do to persuade him to let me find out Miss Morstan's address and send her a detached pearl at fixed intervals, so that at least she might never feel **destitute**."

"It was a kindly thought," said our companion, earnestly. "It was extremely good of you."

The little man waved his hand **deprecatingly**.

deprecatingly [déprikèitiŋli] adv. 부정하듯이, 겸손하여
trustee [trʌstí:] n. 수탁자, 보관자
scurvy [skə́:rvi] adj. 천한, 상스러운
Le mauvais goût mène au crime:
(French) 악취미는 범죄로 이어지게 마련이다
lodge [lɑdʒ / lɔdʒ] n. 별장, 저택

"We were your **trustees**," he said. "That was the view which I took of it, though Brother Bartholomew could not altogether see it in that light. We had plenty of money ourselves. I desired no more. Besides, it would have been such bad taste to have treated a young lady in so **scurvy** a fashion. '*Le mauvais goût mène au crime*.' The French have a very neat way of putting these things. Our difference of opinion on this subject went so far that I thought it best to set up rooms for myself: so I left Pondicherry **Lodge**, taking the old khitmutgar and Williams with me. Yesterday, however, I learn that an event of extreme importance has occurred. The treasure has been discovered. I instantly communicated with Miss

## 4 The Story of the Bald-Headed Man

Morstan, and it only remains for us to drive out to Norwood and demand our share. I explained my views last night to Brother Bartholomew: so we shall be expected, if not welcome, visitors."

Mr. Thaddeus Sholto ceased, and sat **twitching** on his luxurious settee. We all remained silent, with our thoughts upon the new development which the mysterious business had taken. Holmes was the first to spring to his feet.

"You have done well, sir, from first to last," said he. "It is possible that we may be able to make you some small return by throwing some light upon that which is still dark to you. But, as Miss Morstan remarked just now, it is late, and we had best put the matter through without delay."

Our new **acquaintance** very deliberately coiled up the tube of his hookah, and produced from behind a curtain a very long befrogged topcoat with Astrakhan collar and cuffs. This he buttoned tightly up, in spite of the extreme closeness of the night, and finished his **attire** by putting on a rabbit-skin cap with hanging **lappets** which covered the ears, so that no part of him was visible save his mobile and **peaky** face.

"My health is somewhat **fragile**," he remarked, as he led the way down the passage. "I am compelled to be a **valetudinarian**."

Our cab was awaiting us outside, and our programme was evidently prearranged, for the driver started off at once at a rapid pace. Thaddeus Sholto talked **incessantly**, in a voice which rose high above the rattle of the wheels.

"Bartholomew is a clever fellow," said he. "How

unaccounted for:
설명이 되지 않은, 원인 불명의
ascertain [æ̀sərtéin] v.
확인하다, 밝혀내다
lath [læθ, lɑ:θ] n.
외, 욋가지 (지붕이나 벽에 흙을 바르기 위해 엮어넣는 가느다란 나뭇가지)
garret [gǽrət] n.
다락방
rafter [rǽftə:r, rá:ftə:r] n.
서까래, 들보
sterling [stə́:rliŋ]
stg. 영국 화폐, 파운드

could we: if we could
needy [ní:di] adj.
가난한
heiress [ɛ́əris] n.
여자 상속인
rejoice [ridʒɔ́is] v.
기뻐하다
downcast [ˈ-kæ̀st / ˈ-kɑ̀:st] adj.
의기 소침한, 고개를 숙인
babble [bǽbəl] n.
허튼 소리, 잡담
hypochondriac [hàipəkɑ́ndriæ̀k / -kɔn-] n.
심기증 (心氣症) 환자

do you think he found out where the treasure was? He had come to the conclusion that it was somewhere indoors: so he worked out all the cubic space of the house, and made measurements everywhere, so that not one inch should be **unaccounted for**. Among other things, he found that the height of the building was seventy-four feet, but on adding together the heights of all the separate rooms, and making every allowance for the space between, which he **ascertained** by borings, he could not bring the total to more than seventy feet. There were four feet unaccounted for. These could only be at the top of the building. He knocked a hole, therefore, in the **lath**-and-plaster ceiling of the highest room, and there, sure enough, he came upon another little **garret** above it, which had been sealed up and was known to no one. In the centre stood the treasure-chest, resting upon two **rafters**. He lowered it through the hole, and there it lies. He computes the value of the jewels at not less than half a million **sterling**."

At the mention of this gigantic sum we all stared at one another open-eyed. Miss Morstan, **could we** secure her rights, would change from a **needy** governess to the richest **heiress** in England. Surely it was the place of a loyal friend to **rejoice** at such news; yet I am ashamed to say that selfishness took me by the soul, and that my heart turned as heavy as lead within me. I stammered out some few halting words of congratulation, and then sat **downcast**, with my head drooped, deaf to the **babble** of our new acquaintance. He was clearly a confirmed **hypochondriac**, and I was dreamily

## 4 The Story of the Bald-Headed Man

interminable [intə́ːrmənəbəl] adj. 끝없는, 계속되는
implore [implɔ́ːr] v. 간청하다
innumerable [injúːmərəbəl] adj. 무수한, 셀 수 없이 많은
quack [kwæk] adj. 돌팔이의, 엉터리의
nostrum [nástrəm / nɔ́s-] n. 엉터리약, 묘약

conscious that he was pouring forth **interminable** trains of symptoms, and **imploring** information as to the composition and action of **innumerable quack nostrums**, some of which he bore about in a leather case in his pocket. I trust that he may not remember any of the answers which I gave him that night. Holmes declares that he overheard me caution him against the great danger of taking more than two drops of castor oil, while I recommended strychnine in large doses as a sedative. However that may be, I was certainly relieved when our cab pulled up with a jerk and the coachman sprang down to open the door.

"This, Miss Morstan, is Pondicherry Lodge," said Mr. Thaddeus Sholto, as he handed her out.

# 5 The Tragedy of Pondicherry Lodge

damp [dæmp] adj.
습기 있는
rift: [rift] n.
갈라진 틈

It was nearly eleven o'clock when we reached this final stage of our night's adventures. We had left the **damp** fog of the great city behind us, and the night was fairly fine. A warm wind blew from the westward, and heavy clouds moved slowly across the sky, with half a moon peeping occasionally through the **rifts**. It was clear enough to see for some distance, but Thaddeus Sholto took down one of the side-lamps from the carriage to give us a better light upon our way.

lodge [lɑdʒ / lɔdʒ] n.
별장, 저택
gird [gə:rd] v.
(gird - girded or girt)
둘러싸다

Pondicherry **Lodge** stood in its own grounds, and was **girt** round with a very high stone wall topped with broken glass. A single narrow iron-clamped door formed the only means of entrance. On this our guide knocked with a peculiar postman-like

## 5 The Tragedy of Pondicherry Lodge

rat-tat [rǽttǽt] n.
(문 등을) 두드리는 소리
gruff [grʌf] adj.
거친, 걸걸한

clanking [klǽŋkiŋ] n.
철컹 소리, 금속성 소리
jarring [dʒɑ:riŋ] n.
삐걱거리는 소리
distrustful [distrʌ́stfəl] adj.
의심스러운, 믿지 않는

ain't: has not
o': of

perplexed [pərplékst] adj.
당황한

inexorably [inéksərəbəli] adv.
가차없이, 용서없이

genially [dʒí:njəli] adv.
온화하게, 다정하게

**rat-tat**.

"Who is there?" cried a **gruff** voice from within.

"It is I, McMurdo. You surely know my knock by this time."

There was a grumbling sound and a **clanking** and **jarring** of keys. The door swung heavily back, and a short, deep-chested man stood in the opening, with the yellow light of the lantern shining upon his protruded face and twinkling **distrustful** eyes.

"That you, Mr. Thaddeus? But who are the others? I had no orders about them from the master."

"No, McMurdo? You surprise me! I told my brother last night that I should bring some friends."

"He **ain't** been out **o'** his room to-day, Mr. Thaddeus, and I have no orders. You know very well that I must stick to regulations. I can let you in, but your friends must just stop where they are."

This was an unexpected obstacle. Thaddeus Sholto looked about him in a **perplexed** and helpless manner.

This is too bad of you, McMurdo!" he said. "If I guarantee them, that is enough for you. There is the young lady, too. She cannot wait on the public road at this hour."

"Very sorry, Mr. Thaddeus," said the porter, **inexorably**. "Folk may be friends o' yours, and yet no friends o' the master's. He pays me well to do my duty, and my duty I'll do. I don't know none o' your friends."

"Oh, yes you do, McMurdo," cried Sherlock Holmes, **genially**. "I don't think you can have forgotten me. Don't you remember the amateur who fought three rounds with you at Alison's rooms on the night of your benefit four years back?"

"Not Mr. Sherlock Holmes!" roared the prize-fighter. "God's truth! how could I have mistook you? If instead o' standin' there so quiet you had just stepped up and given me that cross-hit of yours under the jaw, I'd ha' known you without a question. Ah, you're one that has wasted your gifts, you have! You might have aimed high, if you had joined the fancy."

"You see, Watson, if all else fails me I have still one of the scientific professions open to me," said Holmes, laughing. "Our friend won't keep us out in the cold now, I am sure."

"In you come, sir, in you come,—you and your friends," he answered. "Very sorry, Mr. Thaddeus,

"Not Mr. Sherlock Holmes!" roared the prize-fighter.

but orders are very strict. Had to be certain of your friends before I let them in."

Inside, a gravel path wound through **desolate** grounds to a huge clump of a house, square and **prosaic**, all plunged in shadow save where a moonbeam struck one corner and glimmered in a garret window. The vast size of the building, with its gloom and its deathly silence, struck a chill to the heart. Even Thaddeus Sholto seemed **ill at ease**, and the lantern quivered and rattled in his hand.

"I cannot understand it," he said. "There must be some mistake. I distinctly told Bartholomew that we should be here, and yet there is no light in his window. I do not know what to **make of** it."

"Does he always guard the **premises** in this way?" asked Holmes.

"Yes; he has followed my father's custom. He was the favorite son, you know, and I sometimes think that my father may have told him more than he ever told me. That is Bartholomew's window up there where the moonshine strikes. It is quite bright, but there is no light from within, I think."

"None," said Holmes. "But I see the **glint** of a light in that little window beside the door."

"Ah, that is the housekeeper's room. That is where old Mrs. Bernstone sits. She can tell us all about it. But perhaps you would not mind waiting here for a minute or two, for if we all go in together and she has no word of our coming she may be alarmed. But hush! what is that?"

He held up the lantern, and his hand shook until the circles of light **flickered** and **wavered** all round us. Miss Morstan seized my wrist, and we all stood with thumping hearts, straining our ears. From the great black house there sounded through the silent night the saddest and most pitiful of sounds,—the shrill, broken whimpering of a frightened woman.

"It is Mrs. Bernstone," said Sholto. "She is the only woman in the house. Wait here. I shall be back in a moment." He hurried for the door, and knocked in his peculiar way. We could see a tall old woman admit him, and sway with pleasure at the very sight of him.

"Oh, Mr. Thaddeus, sir, I am so glad you have come! I am so glad you have come, Mr. Thaddeus, sir!"

We heard her reiterated rejoicings until the door was closed and her voice died away into a muffled monotone.

Our guide had left us the lantern. Holmes swung it slowly round, and peered keenly at the house, and at the great rubbish-heaps which **cumbered** the grounds. Miss Morstan and I stood together, and her hand was in mine. A wondrous subtle thing is love, for here were we two who had never seen each other before that day, between whom no word or even look of affection had ever passed, and yet now in an hour of trouble our hands instinctively sought for each other. I have marvelled at it since, but at the time it seemed the most natural thing that I should go out to her so, and, as she has often told me, there was in her also the instinct to turn to me for comfort and protection. So we stood hand in hand, like two children, and there was peace in our hearts for all the dark things

---

cumber [kʌ́mbər] v.
거치적거리다

So we stood hand in hand, like two children, and there was peace in our hearts for all the dark things that surrounded us.

that surrounded us.

"What a strange place!" she said, looking round.

"It looks as though all the moles in England had been let loose in it. I have seen something of the sort on the side of a hill near Ballarat, where the **prospectors** had been at work."

"And from the same cause," said Holmes. "These are the traces of the treasure-seekers. You must remember that they were six years looking for it. No wonder that the grounds look like a **gravel-pit**."

At that moment the door of the house burst open, and Thaddeus Sholto came running out, with his hands thrown forward and terror in his eyes.

"There is something **amiss** with Bartholomew!" he cried. "I am frightened! My nerves cannot stand it."

He was, indeed, half **blubbering** with fear, and his twitching feeble face peeping out from the great Astrakhan collar had the helpless appealing expression of a terrified child.

"Come into the house," said Holmes, in his crisp, firm way.

"Yes, do!" pleaded Thaddeus Sholto. "I really do not feel equal to giving directions."

We all followed him into the housekeeper's room, which stood upon the left-hand side of the passage. The old woman was pacing up and down with a scared look and restless picking fingers, but the sight of Miss Morstan appeared to have a **soothing** effect upon her.

"God bless your sweet calm face!" she cried, with an hysterical sob.

---

prospector [práspektər / prəspék-] n.
광맥이나 석유 등을 찾는 사람, 시굴자, 탐광자

gravel pit:
자갈 채취장, 자갈 구덩이

amiss [əmís] adj.
잘못된, 정상이 아닌

blubber [blʎbər] v.
울며 말하다

soothing [súːðiŋ] adj.
진정시키는, 누그러뜨리는

"It does me good to see you. Oh, but I have been sorely tried this day!"

Our companion patted her thin, work-worn hand, and **murmured** some few words of kindly, womanly comfort, which brought the color back into the other's bloodless cheeks.

"Master has locked himself in, and will not answer me," she explained.

"All day I have waited to hear from him, for he often likes to be alone; but an hour ago I feared that something was amiss, so I went up and peeped through the key-hole. You must go up, Mr. Thaddeus,—you must go up and look for yourself. I have seen Mr. Bartholomew Sholto, in joy and in sorrow for ten long years, but I never saw him with such a face on him as that."

Sherlock Holmes took the lamp and led the way, for Thaddeus Sholto's teeth were chattering in his head. So shaken was he that I had to pass my hand under his arm as we went up the stairs, for his knees were trembling under him. Twice as we ascended Holmes whipped his lens out of his pocket and carefully examined marks which appeared to me to be mere shapeless **smudges** of dust upon the cocoa-nut matting which served as a stair-carpet. He walked slowly from step to step, holding the lamp low, and shooting keen glances to right and left. Miss Morstan had remained behind with the frightened housekeeper.

The third flight of stairs ended in a straight passage of some length, with a great picture in Indian tapestry upon the right of it and three doors upon the left. Holmes advanced along it in the same slow and methodical way, while we kept close at his heels, with our long black shadows streaming backwards down the corridor. The third door was that which we were seeking. Holmes knocked without receiving any answer, and then tried to turn the handle and force it open. It was locked on the inside, however, and by a broad and powerful bolt, as we could see when we set our lamp up against it. The key being turned, however, the hole was not entirely closed. Sherlock Holmes bent down to it, and instantly rose again with a sharp intaking of the breath.

"There is something devilish in this, Watson," said he, more moved than I had ever before seen him. "What do you make of it?"

I stooped to the hole, and **recoiled** in horror. Moonlight was streaming into the room, and it was bright with a vague and shifty radiance. Looking straight at me, and suspended, as it were, in the air, for all beneath was in shadow, there hung a face,—the very face of our companion Thaddeus. There was the same high, shining head, the same circular bristle of red hair, the same bloodless **countenance**. The features were set, however, in a horrible smile, a fixed and unnatural grin, which in that still and moonlit room was more **jarring** to the nerves than any **scowl** or **contortion**. So like was the face to that of our little friend that I looked round at him to make sure that he was indeed with us. Then I recalled to mind that he had mentioned to us that his brother and he were twins.

"This is terrible!" I said to Holmes. "What is

---

recoil [rikɔ́il, ríːkɔ̀il] v.
물러나다, 후퇴하다, 반동하다
countenance [káuntənəns] n.
얼굴 표정, 안색
jarring [dʒɑːriŋ] n.
동요, 충격
scowl [skaul] n.
찡그린 얼굴
contortion [kəntɔ́ːrʃən] n.
일그러짐

**come down:**
넘어지다, 쓰러지다

**groan** [groun] v.
삐걱거리다
**fling** [fliŋ] v.
to throw, hurl

**retort** [ritɔ́:rt] n.
증류기
**carboy** [ká:rbɔi] n.
상자 등에 보관하는 내산(耐酸)병
**wicker** [wíkəːr] n.
(버드나무의) 작은 가지, 고리버들 세공품
**pungent** [pʌ́ndʒənt] adj.
자극성이 강한

**ghastly** [gǽstli / gáː·st-] adj.
창백한, 무시무시한
**inscrutable** [inskrúːtəbəl] adj.
알 수 없는, 불가사의한
**close-grained** [klóusgréind] adj.
결이 고운, 촘촘한

to be done?"

"The door must **come down**," he answered, and, springing against it, he put all his weight upon the lock.

It creaked and **groaned**, but did not yield. Together we **flung** ourselves upon it once more, and this time it gave way with a sudden snap, and we found ourselves within Bartholomew Sholto's chamber.

It appeared to have been fitted up as a chemical laboratory. A double line of glass-stoppered bottles was drawn up upon the wall opposite the door, and the table was littered over with Bunsen burners, test-tubes, and **retorts**. In the corners stood **carboys** of acid in **wicker** baskets. One of these appeared to leak or to have been broken, for a stream of dark-colored liquid had trickled out from it, and the air was heavy with a peculiarly **pungent**, tar-like odor. A set of steps stood at one side of the room, in the midst of a litter of lath and plaster, and above them there was an opening in the ceiling large enough for a man to pass through. At the foot of the steps a long coil of rope was thrown carelessly together.

By the table, in a wooden arm-chair, the master of the house was seated all in a heap, with his head sunk upon his left shoulder, and that **ghastly**, **inscrutable** smile upon his face. He was stiff and cold, and had clearly been dead many hours. It seemed to me that not only his features but all his limbs were twisted and turned in the most fantastic fashion. By his hand upon the table there lay a peculiar instrument,—a brown, **close-grained** stick, with a stone head like a hammer, rudely **lashed** on with coarse **twine**. Beside it was a torn sheet of note-paper with some words scrawled upon it. Holmes glanced at it, and then handed it to me.

"You see," he said, with a significant raising of the eyebrows.

In the light of the lantern I read, with a thrill of horror, "The sign of the four."

"In God's name, what does it all mean?" I asked.

"It means murder," said he, stooping over the dead man. "Ah, I expected it. Look here!"

He pointed to what looked like a long, dark thorn stuck in the skin just above the ear.

"It looks like a thorn," said I.

"It is a thorn. You may pick it out. But be careful,

for it is poisoned."

I took it up between my finger and thumb. It came away from the skin so readily that hardly any mark was left behind. One tiny speck of blood showed where the puncture had been.

"This is all an **insoluble** mystery to me," said I. "It grows darker instead of clearer."

"On the contrary," he answered, "it clears every instant. I only require a few missing links to have an entirely connected case."

We had almost forgotten our companion's presence since we entered the chamber. He was still standing in the door-way, the very picture of terror, wringing his hands and **moaning** to himself. Suddenly, however, he broke out into a sharp, **querulous** cry.

"The treasure is gone!" he said. "They have robbed him of the treasure! There is the hole through which we lowered it. I helped him to do it! I was the last person who saw him! I left him here last night, and I heard him lock the door as I came down-stairs."

"What time was that?"

"It was ten o'clock. And now he is dead, and the police will be called in, and I shall be suspected of having had a hand in it. Oh, yes, I am sure I shall. But you don't think so, gentlemen? Surely you don't think that it was I? Is it likely that I would have brought you here if it were I? Oh, dear! oh, dear! I know that I shall go mad!"

He jerked his arms and stamped his feet in a kind of **convulsive frenzy**.

"You have no reason for fear, Mr. Sholto," said

Holmes, kindly, putting his hand upon his shoulder. "Take my advice, and drive down to the station to report this matter to the police. Offer to assist them in every way. We shall wait here until your return."

The little man obeyed in a half-stupefied fashion, and we heard him stumbling down the stairs in the dark.

# 6 Sherlock Holmes Gives a Demonstration

err [ə:r, ɛər] v.
틀리다, 잘못 생각하다

"Now, Watson," said Holmes, rubbing his hands, "we have half an hour to ourselves. Let us make good use of it. My case is, as I have told you, almost complete; but we must not **err** on the side of over-confidence. Simple as the case seems now, there may be something deeper underlying it."

"Simple!" I ejaculated.

expound [ikspáund] v.
설명하다

mutter [mʌ́tə:r] v.
낮고 불명확한 소리로 말하다, 중얼중얼 말하다

"Surely," said he, with something of the air of a clinical professor **expounding** to his class. "Just sit in the corner there, that your footprints may not complicate matters. Now to work! In the first place, how did these folk come, and how did they go? The door has not been opened since last night. How of the window?" He carried the lamp across to it, **muttering** his observations aloud the while,

## 6 Sherlock Holmes Gives a Demonstration

snib [snib] v.
걸쇠를 걸다

stump [stʌmp] n.
의족 義足

ally [əlái, ǽlai] n.
공범, 동료
scale [skeil] v.
기어오르다
foothold [fúthòuld] n.
발판,
crevice [krévis] n.
갈라진 틈

stout [staut] adj.
튼튼한, 견고한
swarm [swɔːrm] v.
기어오르다

but addressing them to himself rather than to me. "Window is **snibbed** on the inner side. Framework is solid. No hinges at the side. Let us open it. No water-pipe near. Roof quite out of reach. Yet a man has mounted by the window. It rained a little last night. Here is the print of a foot in mould upon the sill. And here is a circular muddy mark, and here again upon the floor, and here again by the table. See here, Watson! This is really a very pretty demonstration."

I looked at the round, well-defined muddy discs.

"That is not a footmark," said I.

"It is something much more valuable to us. It is the impression of a wooden **stump**. You see here on the sill is the boot-mark, a heavy boot with the broad metal heel, and beside it is the mark of the timber-toe."

"It is the wooden-legged man."

"Quite so. But there has been some one else,—a very able and efficient **ally**. Could you **scale** that wall, doctor?"

I looked out of the open window. The moon still shone brightly on that angle of the house. We were a good sixty feet from the ground, and, look where I would, I could see no **foothold**, nor as much as a **crevice** in the brick-work.

"It is absolutely impossible," I answered.

"Without aid it is so. But suppose you had a friend up here who lowered you this good **stout** rope which I see in the corner, securing one end of it to this great hook in the wall. Then, I think, if you were an active man, You might **swarm** up, wooden leg and all. You would depart, of course,

**horny** [hɔ́ːrni] adj.
거친, 굳어진, 단단한
**gather** [gǽðər] v.
추측하다

**unintelligible** [ʌ̀nintéləd ʒəbəl]
adj. 알기 힘든, 난해한

**break ground:**
새로 개척하다, 첫삽을 뜨다
**annals** [ǽnəlz] n.
연대기
**Senegambia:**
세네갈과 감비아 강 사이의 서
아프리카 지역

**inaccessible** [inəksésəbəl] adj.
접근하기 어려운

**grate** [greit] n.
(난로 등의) 격자, 창살v

**precept** [príːsept] n.
규칙

in the same fashion, and your ally would draw up the rope, untie it from the hook, shut the window, snib it on the inside, and get away in the way that he originally came. As a minor point it may be noted," he continued, fingering the rope, "that our wooden-legged friend, though a fair climber, was not a professional sailor. His hands were far from **horny**. My lens discloses more than one blood-mark, especially towards the end of the rope, from which I **gather** that he slipped down with such velocity that he took the skin off his hand."

"This is all very well," said I, "but the thing becomes more **unintelligible** than ever. How about this mysterious ally? How came he into the room?"

"Yes, the ally!" repeated Holmes, pensively. "There are features of interest about this ally. He lifts the case from the regions of the commonplace. I fancy that this ally **breaks fresh ground** in the **annals** of crime in this country,—though parallel cases suggest themselves from India, and, if my memory serves me, from **Senegambia**."

"How came he, then?" I reiterated. "The door is locked, the window is **inaccessible**. Was it through the chimney?"

"The **grate** is much too small," he answered. "I had already considered that possibility."

"How then?" I persisted.

"You will not apply my **precept**," he said, shaking his head. "How often have I said to you that when you have eliminated the impossible whatever remains, *however improbable*, must be the truth? We know that he did not come through the door, the window, or the chimney. We also know that he could not have been concealed in the room, as there is no concealment possible. Whence, then, did he come?"

"He came through the hole in the roof," I cried.

"Of course he did. He must have done so. If you will have the kindness to hold the lamp for me, we shall now extend our researches to the room above,—the secret room in which the treasure was found."

He mounted the steps, and, seizing a rafter with either hand, he swung himself up into the garret. Then, lying on his face, he reached down for the lamp and held it while I followed him.

The chamber in which we found ourselves was about ten feet one way and six the other. The floor was formed by the rafters, with thin lath-and-plaster between, so that in walking one had to step from beam to beam. The roof ran up to an apex, and was evidently the inner shell of the true roof of the house. There was no furniture of any sort, and the accumulated dust of years lay thick upon the floor.

"Here you are, you see," said Sherlock Holmes, putting his hand against the sloping wall. "This is a **trap-door** which leads out on to the roof. I can press it back, and here is the roof itself, sloping at a gentle angle. This, then, is the way by which **Number One** entered. Let us see if we can find any other traces of his individuality."

He held down the lamp to the floor, and as he did so I saw for the second time that night a startled, surprised look come over his face. For myself, as I followed his gaze my skin was cold

---

trapdoor n.
통풍문
number one:
중심인물, 주요인물, 이 경우 주요 용의자

scarce [skɛəːrs] adv.
거의 ~ 아닌

horrid [hɔ́ːrid, hár-] adj.
무서운, 무시무시한

stagger [stǽgəːr] v.
흔들리다, 동요하다
foretell [fɔːrtél] v.
예언하다

under my clothes. The floor was covered thickly with the prints of a naked foot,—clear, well defined, perfectly formed, but **scarce** half the size of those of an ordinary man.

"Holmes," I said, in a whisper, "a child has done the **horrid** thing."

He had recovered his self-possession in an instant.

"I was **staggered** for the moment," he said, "but the thing is quite natural. My memory failed me, or I should have been able to **foretell** it. There is nothing more to be learned here. Let us go down."

"What is your theory, then, as to those foot-marks?" I asked, eagerly, when we had regained the lower room once more.

"My dear Watson, try a little analysis yourself," said he, with a touch of impatience. "You know my methods. Apply them, and it will be instructive to compare results."

"I cannot conceive anything which will cover the facts," I answered.

"It will be clear enough to you soon," he said, in an off-hand way. "I think that there is nothing else of importance here, but I will look."

He whipped out his lens and a tape measure, and hurried about the room on his knees, measuring, comparing, examining, with his long thin nose only a few inches from the planks, and his beady eyes gleaming and deep-set like those of a bird. So swift, silent, and **furtive** were his movements, like those of a trained blood-hound picking out a scent, that I could not but think what a terrible criminal he would have made **had he turned** his energy and **sagacity** against the law, instead of exerting them in its defense. As he hunted about, he kept muttering to himself, and finally he broke out into a loud **crow** of delight.

"We are certainly in luck," said he. "We ought to have very little trouble now. Number One has had the misfortune to tread in the **creosote**. You can see the outline of the edge of his small foot here at the side of this evil-smelling mess. The carboy has been cracked, You see, and the stuff has leaked out."

"What then?" I asked.

"Why, we have got him, that's all," said he. "I know a dog that would follow that scent to the world's end. If a **pack** can track a trailed herring

---

furtive [fə́:rtiv] adj.
은밀한,
had he turned:
if he had turned
sagacity [səgǽsəti] n.
현명함
crow [krou] n.
환성

creosote [krí(:)əsòut] n.
크레오소트, 보존방부제

pack [pæk] n.
동물의 한떼

|  |  |
|---|---|
| shire [ʃáiər] n. 예전 영국의 행정구역 | |
| pungent [pʌ́ndʒənt] adj. 자극성이 강한 | |
| accredited [əkréditid] adj. 공인된 | |
| representative [rèprizéntətiv] n. 대표자, 대리인 | |
| clamor [klǽmər] n. 함성, 와글거림 | |
| rigor mortisis [rígə:rmɔ́:rtis / ráigɔ:r] 사후경직 | |
| Hippocratic: 히포크라테스의 | |
| risus sardonicus: sardonic grin 경련 미소 | |
| tetanus [tét-ənəs] n. 지속적 경련 | |
| system [sístəm] n. 인간의 몸, 신체 | |
| gingerly [dʒíndʒərli] adv. 신중하게, 조심해서 | |

across a **shire**, how far can a specially-trained hound follow so **pungent** a smell as this? It sounds like a sum in the rule of three. The answer should give us the—But halloo! here are the **accredited representatives** of the law."

Heavy steps and the **clamor** of loud voices were audible from below, and the hall door shut with a loud crash.

"Before they come," said Holmes, "just put your hand here on this poor fellow's arm, and here on his leg. What do you feel?"

"The muscles are as hard as a board," I answered.

"Quite so. They are in a state of extreme contraction, far exceeding the usual *rigor mortis*. Coupled with this distortion of the face, this **Hippocratic** smile, or '*risus sardonicus*,' as the old writers called it, what conclusion would it suggest to your mind?"

"Death from some powerful vegetable alkaloid," I answered,—"some strychnine-like substance which would produce **tetanus**."

"That was the idea which occurred to me the instant I saw the drawn muscles of the face. On getting into the room I at once looked for the means by which the poison had entered the **system**. As you saw, I discovered a thorn which had been driven or shot with no great force into the scalp. You observe that the part struck was that which would be turned towards the hole in the ceiling if the man were erect in his chair. Now examine the thorn."

I took it up **gingerly** and held it in the light of the lantern. It was long, sharp, and black, with a

## 6 Sherlock Holmes Gives a Demonstration

**glazed** look near the point as though some gummy substance had dried upon it. The blunt end had been trimmed and rounded off with a knife.

"Is that an English thorn?" he asked.

"No, it certainly is not."

"With all these data you should be able to draw some just inference. But here are the **regulars**: so the **auxiliary** forces may **beat a retreat**."

As he spoke, the steps which had been coming nearer sounded loudly on the passage, and a very stout, portly man in a gray suit strode heavily into the room. He was red-faced, **burly** and **plethoric**, with a pair of very small twinkling eyes which looked keenly out from between swollen and puffy pouches. He was closely followed by an inspector in uniform, and by the still palpitating Thaddeus Sholto.

"Here's a business!" he cried, in a muffled, husky voice. "Here's a pretty business! But who are all these? Why, the house seems to be as full as a rabbit-warren!"

"I think you must recollect me, Mr. Athelney Jones," said Holmes, quietly.

"Why, of course I do!" he **wheezed**. "It's Mr. Sherlock Holmes, the **theorist**. Remember you! I'll never forget how you lectured us all on causes and inferences and effects in the Bishopgate jewel case. It's true you set us on the right track; but you'll **own** now that it was more by good luck than good guidance."

"It was a piece of very simple reasoning."

"Oh, come, now, come! Never be ashamed to own up. But what is all this? Bad business! Bad

room [ru:m, rum] n.
여지, 경우, 가능성

hit the nail on the head:
정확하다, 적절한 말을 하다
dear me (also oh dear):
놀람, 동정, 실망 등을 나타내
는 감탄사

fit [fit] n.
발작, 경련

business! Stern facts here,—no **room** for theories. How lucky that I happened to be out at Norwood over another case! I was at the station when the message arrived. What d'you think the man died of?"

"Oh, this is hardly a case for me to theorize over," said Holmes, dryly.

"No, no. Still, we can't deny that you **hit the nail on the head** sometimes. **Dear me**! Door locked, I understand. Jewels worth half a million missing. How was the window?"

"Fastened; but there are steps on the sill."

"Well, well, if it was fastened the steps could have nothing to do with the matter. That's common sense. Man might have died in a **fit**; but then the jewels are missing. Ha! I have a theory. These

flashes come upon me at times.—Just step outside, sergeant, and you, Mr. Sholto. Your friend can remain.—What do you think of this, Holmes? Sholto was, on his own confession, with his brother last night. The brother died in a fit, on which Sholto walked off with the treasure. How's that?"

"On which the dead man very considerately got up and locked the door on the inside."

"Hum! There's a flaw there. Let us apply common sense to the matter. This Thaddeus Sholto *was* with his brother; there *was* a quarrel; so much we know. The brother is dead and the jewels are gone. So much also we know. No one saw the brother from the time Thaddeus left him. His bed had not been slept in. Thaddeus is evidently in a most disturbed state of mind. His appearance is—well, not attractive. You see that I am weaving my web round Thaddeus. The net begins to close upon him."

"You are not quite in possession of the facts yet," said Holmes. "This **splinter** of wood, which I have every reason to believe to be poisoned, was in the man's **scalp** where you still see the mark; this card, inscribed as you see it, was on the table; and beside it lay this rather curious stone-headed instrument. How does all that fit into your theory?"

"Confirms it in every respect," said the fat detective, **pompously**.

"House is full of Indian curiosities. Thaddeus brought this up, and if this splinter be poisonous Thaddeus may as well have made murderous use of it as any other man. The card is some **hocus-pocus**,—a **blind**, as like as not. The only question is,

---

"... The brother died in a fit, on which Sholto walked off with the treasure. How's that?"
"On which the dead man very considerately got up and locked the door on the inside."

splinter [splíntə:r] n.
파편
scalp [skælp] n.
두피, 머리피부

pompously [pámpəsli / pɔ́m-]
adv. 오만하게, 뽐내듯이
hocus-pocus hóukəspóukəs] n.
속임수
blind [blaind] n.
눈속임, 숨기는 수단

how did he depart? Ah, of course, here is a hole in the roof."

With great activity, considering his bulk, he sprang up the steps and squeezed through into the garret, and immediately afterwards we heard his exulting voice proclaiming that he had found the trap-door.

"He can find something," remarked Holmes, shrugging his shoulders. "He has occasional glimmerings of reason. **Il n'y a pas** *des sots si incommodes que ceux qui ont de l'esprit!*"

"You see!" said Athelney Jones, reappearing down the steps again; "facts are better than theories, after all. My view of the case is confirmed. There is a trap-door communicating with the roof, and it is partly open."

"It was I who opened it."

"Oh, indeed! You did notice it, then?" He seemed a little **crestfallen** at the discovery. "Well, whoever noticed it, it shows how our gentleman got away. Inspector!"

"Yes, sir," from the passage.

"Ask Mr. Sholto to step this way.—Mr. Sholto, it is my duty to inform you that anything which you may say will be used against you. I arrest you in the Queen's name as being concerned in the death of your brother."

"There, now! Didn't I tell you!" cried the poor little man, throwing out his hands, and looking from one to the other of us.

"Don't trouble yourself about it, Mr. Sholto," said Holmes. "I think that I can **engage** to clear you of the charge."

## 6 Sherlock Holmes Gives a Demonstration

"Don't promise too much, Mr. Theorist,—don't promise too much!" snapped the detective. "You may find it a harder matter than you think."

"Not only will I clear him, Mr. Jones, but I will make you a free present of the name and description of one of the two people who were in this room last night. His name, I have every reason to believe, is Jonathan Small. He is a poorly-educated man, small, active, with his right leg off, and wearing a wooden stump which is worn away upon the inner side. His left boot has a coarse, square-toed sole, with an iron band round the heel. He is a middle-aged man, much sunburned, and has been a convict. These few indications may be of some assistance to you, coupled with the fact that there is a good deal of skin missing from the palm of his hand. The other man—"

"Ah! the other man—?" asked Athelney Jones, in a sneering voice, but impressed **none the less**, as I could easily see, by the precision of the other's manner.

"Is a rather curious person," said Sherlock Holmes, turning upon his heel. "I hope before very long to be able to introduce you to the pair of them.—A word with you, Watson."

He led me out to the head of the stair.

"This unexpected occurrence," he said, "has caused us rather to lose sight of the original purpose of our journey."

"I have just been thinking so," I answered. "It is not right that Miss Morstan should remain in this **stricken** house."

"No. You must escort her home. She lives with

---

"...His name, I have every reason to believe, is Jonathan Small..."

none the less:
그럼에도 불구하고, 그래도 역시

stricken [strík-ən] adj.
피해를 입은

by no means:
절대 아닌

exult [igzʌ́lt] v.
기뻐하다
mare's nest [méə:rznèst]
속임수
compliment [kámpləmənt / kɔ́m-] n.
안부, 인사

mongrel [mʌ́ŋgrəl, mɑ́ŋ-] n.
잡종개

Mrs. Cecil Forrester, in Lower Camberwell: so it is not very far. I will wait for you here if you will drive out again. Or perhaps you are too tired?"

"**By no means.** I don't think I could rest until I know more of this fantastic business. I have seen something of the rough side of life, but I give you my word that this quick succession of strange surprises to-night has shaken my nerve completely. I should like, however, to see the matter through with you, now that I have got so far."

"Your presence will be of great service to me," he answered. "We shall work the case out independently, and leave this fellow Jones to **exult** over any **mare's-nest** which he may choose to construct. When you have dropped Miss Morstan I wish you to go on to No. 3 Pinchin Lane, down near the water's edge at Lambeth. The third house on the right-hand side is a bird-stuffer's: Sherman is the name. You will see a weasel holding a young rabbit in the window. Knock old Sherman up, and tell him, with my **compliments**, that I want Toby at once. You will bring Toby back in the cab with you."

"A dog, I suppose."

"Yes,—a queer **mongrel**, with a most amazing power of scent. I would rather have Toby's help than that of the whole detective force of London."

"I shall bring him, then," said I. "It is one now. I ought to be back before three, if I can get a fresh horse."

"And I," said Holmes, "shall see what I can learn from Mrs. Bernstone, and from the Indian servant, who, Mr. Thaddeus tells me, sleeps in the next

sarcasm [sáːrkæz-əm] n.
빈정댐, 비꼼, 풍자
Wir sind gewohnt ~:
(German) 인간은 본인이 이해하지 못하는 것을 낮잡아보는 경향이 있다.
pithy [píθi] adj.
간결하고 명쾌한

garret. Then I shall study the great Jones's methods and listen to his not too delicate **sarcasms**. "*Wir sind gewohnt dass die Menschen verhöhnen was sie nicht verstehen*." Goethe is always **pithy**."

# 7 *The Episode of the Barrel*

placid [plǽsid] adj.
조용한, 평온한
self-restraint [sélfristréint] n.
자제, 극기

The police had brought a cab with them, and in this I escorted Miss Morstan back to her home. After the angelic fashion of women, she had borne trouble with a calm face as long as there was some one weaker than herself to support, and I had found her bright and **placid** by the side of the frightened housekeeper. In the cab, however, she first turned faint, and then burst into a passion of weeping,—so sorely had she been tried by the adventures of the night. She has told me since that she thought me cold and distant upon that journey. She little guessed the struggle within my breast, or the effort of **self-restraint** which held me back. My sympathies and my love went out to her, even as my hand had in the garden. I felt that years of the conventionalities of life could not teach me to know her sweet, brave nature as had this one day of strange experiences. Yet there were two thoughts which sealed the words of affection upon my lips. She was weak and helpless, shaken in mind and nerve. It was to take her at a **disadvantage** to **obtrude** love upon her at such a time. Worse still, she was rich. If Holmes's researches were successful, she would be an heiress. Was it fair, was it honorable, that a half-pay surgeon should take such advantage of an intimacy which chance had brought about? Might she not look upon me as a mere **vulgar** fortune-seeker? I could not bear to risk that such a thought should **cross her mind**. This Agra treasure **intervened** like an **impassable** barrier between us.

It was nearly two o'clock when we reached Mrs. Cecil Forrester's. The servants had retired hours ago, but Mrs. Forrester had been so interested by the strange message which Miss Morstan had received that she had sat up in the hope of her return. She opened the door herself, a middle-aged, graceful woman, and it gave me joy to see how tenderly her arm stole round the other's waist and how motherly was the voice in which she greeted her. She was clearly no mere paid dependant, but an honored friend. I was introduced, and Mrs. Forrester earnestly begged me to step in and tell her our adventures. I explained, however, the importance of my errand, and promised faithfully to call and report any progress which we might make with the case. As we drove away I stole a glance back, and I still seem to see that little group

---

disadvantage [dìsədvǽntidʒ, -vɑ́:n-] n.
불리한 처지
obtrude [əbtrú:d] v.
강요하다
vulgar [vʌ́lgər] adj.
천한, 비속한
cross one's mind:
알게 되다, 깨닫게 되다
intervene [ìntərví:n] v.
끼어들다
impassable [impǽsəbəl, -pɑ́:s-] adj. 지날 수 없는

This Agra treasure intervened like an impassable barrier between us.

glimpse [glimps] n.
언뜻 눈에 띄임
tranquil [trǽŋkwil] adj.
고요한, 평온한, 차분한

singular [síŋgjələ:r] adj.
이상한, 희한한
labyrinth [lǽbərìnə] n.
미로 迷路

vagabond [vǽgəbànd / -bɔ̀n] n.
방랑자, 부랑자

on the step, the two graceful, clinging figures, the half-opened door, the hall light shining through stained glass, the barometer, and the bright stair-rods. It was soothing to catch even that passing **glimpse** of a **tranquil** English home in the midst of the wild, dark business which had absorbed us.

And the more I thought of what had happened, the wilder and darker it grew. I reviewed the whole extraordinary sequence of events as I rattled on through the silent gas-lit streets. There was the original problem: that at least was pretty clear now. The death of Captain Morstan, the sending of the pearls, the advertisement, the letter,—we had had light upon all those events. They had only led us, however, to a deeper and far more tragic mystery. The Indian treasure, the curious plan found among Morstan's baggage, the strange scene at Major Sholto's death, the rediscovery of the treasure immediately followed by the murder of the discoverer, the very **singular** accompaniments to the crime, the footsteps, the remarkable weapons, the words upon the card, corresponding with those upon Captain Morstan's chart,—here was indeed a **labyrinth** in which a man less singularly endowed than my fellow-lodger might well despair of ever finding the clue.

Pinchin Lane was a row of shabby, two-storied brick houses in the lower quarter of Lambeth. I had to knock for some time at No. 3 before I could make any impression. At last, however, there was the glint of a candle behind the blind, and a face looked out at the upper window.

"Go on, you drunken **vagabond**," said the face.

row [rau] n.
소란, 난리법석
kennel [kénəl] n.
개집, 견사

your 'ead: your head

lanky [lǽŋki] adj.
마른, 호리호리한
stringy [stríŋi] adj.
마른

"If you kick up any more **row** I'll open the **kennels** and let out forty-three dogs upon you."

"If you'll let one out, it's just what I have come for," said I.

"Go on!" yelled the voice. "So help me gracious, I have a wiper in the bag, an' I'll drop it on **your 'ead** if you don't hook it."

"But I want a dog," I cried.

"I won't be argued with!" shouted Mr. Sherman. "Now stand clear, for when I say 'three,' down goes the wiper."

"Mr. Sherlock Holmes—" I began, but the words had a most magical effect, for the window instantly slammed down, and within a minute the door was unbarred and open. Mr. Sherman was a **lanky**, lean old man, with stooping shoulders, a **stringy**

naughty [nɔ́:ti, nά:ti] adj.
말을 듣지 않는, 장난을 좋아하는
stoat [stout] n.
(여름털이 갈색인) 족제비
slowworm [´-wə̀:rm] n.
유럽산의 무족 도마뱀
guy [gai] v.
놀리다, 조롱하다

cranny [krǽni] n.
갈라진 틈
slumber [slʌ́mbə:r] n.
잠, 수면

lop-eared [lάpíərd / lɔ́p-] adj.
귀가 처진
naturalist [nǽtʃərəlist] n.
박물학자

neck, and blue-tinted glasses.

"A friend of Mr. Sherlock is always welcome," said he. "Step in, sir. Keep clear of the badger; for he bites. Ah, **naughty**, naughty, would you take a nip at the gentleman?" This to a **stoat** which thrust its wicked head and red eyes between the bars of its cage. "Don't mind that, sir: it's only a **slow-worm**. It hain't got no fangs, so I gives it the run o' the room, for it keeps the beetles down. You must not mind my bein' just a little short wi' you at first, for I'm **guyed** at by the children, and there's many a one just comes down this lane to knock me up. What was it that Mr. Sherlock Holmes wanted, sir?"

"He wanted a dog of yours."

"Ah! that would be Toby."

"Yes, 'Toby' was the name."

"Toby lives at No. 7 on the left here."

He moved slowly forward with his candle among the queer animal family which he had gathered round him. In the uncertain, shadowy light I could see dimly that there were glancing, glimmering eyes peeping down at us from every **cranny** and corner. Even the rafters above our heads were lined by solemn fowls, who lazily shifted their weight from one leg to the other as our voices disturbed their **slumbers**.

Toby proved to be an ugly, long-haired, **lop-eared** creature, half spaniel and half lurcher, brown-and-white in color, with a very clumsy waddling gait. It accepted after some hesitation a lump of sugar which the old **naturalist** handed to me, and, having thus sealed an alliance, it

accessory [æksésəri] n.
공범
constable [kánstəbl / kʌ́n-] n.
순경

bull's eye [búlzài] n.
랜턴
card:
cord의 오식 誤植

clamber [klǽmbər] v.
기어오르다

followed me to the cab, and made no difficulties about accompanying me. It had just struck three on the Palace clock when I found myself back once more at Pondicherry Lodge. The ex-prize-fighter McMurdo had, I found, been arrested as an **accessory**, and both he and Mr. Sholto had been marched off to the station. Two **constables** guarded the narrow gate, but they allowed me to pass with the dog on my mentioning the detective's name.

Holmes was standing on the door-step, with his hands in his pockets, smoking his pipe.

"Ah, you have him there!" said he. "Good dog, then! Athelney Jones has gone. We have had an immense display of energy since you left. He has arrested not only friend Thaddeus, but the gate-keeper, the housekeeper, and the Indian servant. We have the place to ourselves, but for a sergeant up-stairs. Leave the dog here, and come up."

We tied Toby to the hall table, and reascended the stairs. The room was as he had left it, save that a sheet had been draped over the central figure. A weary-looking police-sergeant reclined in the corner.

"Lend me your **bull's-eye**, sergeant," said my companion. "Now tie this bit of **card** round my neck, so as to hang it in front of me. Thank you. Now I must kick off my boots and stockings. Just you carry them down with you, Watson. I am going to do a little climbing. And dip my handkerchief into the creosote. That will do. Now come up into the garret with me for a moment."

We **clambered** up through the hole. Holmes turned his light once more upon the footsteps in

noteworthy [nóutwə̀:rði] adj.
주목할 만한, 현저한, 두드러진

cramp [kræmp] v.
단단히(빈틈없이) 유지하다, (꺾쇠 등으로) 고정시키다
bear in mind:
기억하다

tarry [tá:ri] adj.
타르의, 타르를 바른
Blondin:
Charles Blondin, 19세기 프랑스 곡예사

ridge [ridʒ] n.
지붕의 용마루
eaves [i:vz] n.
처마

the dust.

"I wish you particularly to notice these foot-marks," he said. "Do you observe anything **noteworthy** about them?"

"They belong," I said, "to a child or a small woman."

"Apart from their size, though. Is there nothing else?"

"They appear to be much as other footmarks."

"Not at all. Look here! This is the print of a right foot in the dust. Now I make one with my naked foot beside it. What is the chief difference?"

"Your toes are all **cramped** together. The other print has each toe distinctly divided."

"Quite so. That is the point. **Bear that in mind**. Now, would you kindly step over to that flap-window and smell the edge of the wood-work? I shall stay over here, as I have this handkerchief in my hand."

I did as he directed, and was instantly conscious of a strong **tarry** smell.

"That is where he put his foot in getting out. If you can trace him, I should think that Toby will have no difficulty. Now run down-stairs, loose the dog, and look out for **Blondin**."

By the time that I got out into the grounds Sherlock Holmes was on the roof, and I could see him like an enormous glow-worm crawling very slowly along the **ridge**. I lost sight of him behind a stack of chimneys, but he presently reappeared, and then vanished once more upon the opposite side. When I made my way round there I found him seated at one of the corner **eaves**.

## 7 The Episode of the Barrel

"That you, Watson?" he cried.

"Yes."

"This is the place. What is that black thing down there?"

"A water-barrel."

"Top on it?"

"Yes."

"No sign of a ladder?"

"No."

"Confound the fellow! It's a most **break-neck** place. I ought to be able to come down where he could climb up. The water-pipe feels pretty firm. Here goes, anyhow."

There was a scuffling of feet, and the lantern began to come steadily down the side of the wall. Then with a light spring he came on to the barrel, and from there to the earth.

"It was easy to follow him," he said, drawing on his stockings and boots. "Tiles were loosened the whole way along, and in his hurry he had dropped this. It confirms my diagnosis, as you doctors express it."

The object which he held up to me was a small pocket or pouch woven out of colored grasses and with a few **tawdry** beads strung round it. In shape and size it was not unlike a cigarette-case. Inside were half a dozen **spines** of dark wood, sharp at one end and rounded at the other, like that which had struck Bartholomew Sholto.

"They are **hellish** things," said he. "**Look out** that you don't prick yourself. I'm delighted to have them, for the chances are that they are all he has. There is the less fear of you or me finding

---

breakneck [bréiknèk] adj.
위험한

tawdry [tɔ́:dri] adj.
값싸고 야한
spine [spain] n.
가시

hellish [héliʃ] adj.
지옥 같은, 가증할, 무시무시한
look out:
경계하다, 조심하다

one in our skin before long. I **would sooner** face a Martini bullet, myself. **Are you game** for a six-mile **trudge**, Watson?"

"Certainly," I answered.

"Your leg will stand it?"

"Oh, yes."

"Here you are, doggy! Good old Toby! Smell it, Toby, smell it!" He pushed the creosote handkerchief under the dog's nose, while the creature stood with its fluffy legs separated, and with a most comical cock to its head, like a **connoisseur** sniffing the *bouquet* of a famous vintage. Holmes then threw the handkerchief to a distance, fastened a stout cord to the **mongrel**'s collar, and led him to the foot of the water-barrel. The creature instantly broke into a succession of high, **tremulous yelps**, and, with his nose on the ground, and his tail in the air, **pattered** off upon the trail at a pace which strained his leash and kept us at the top of our speed.

The east had been gradually whitening, and we could now see some distance in the cold gray light. The square, massive house, with its black, empty windows and high, bare walls, towered up, sad and **forlorn**, behind us. Our course led right across the grounds, in and out among the trenches and pits with which they were scarred and intersected. The whole place, with its scattered dirt-heaps and ill-grown shrubs, had a **blighted**, **ill-omened** look which harmonized with the black tragedy which hung over it.

On reaching the boundary wall Toby ran along, whining eagerly, underneath its shadow, and

---

would sooner:
would rather
cf) I would prefer a Martini bullet to the poison darts.
Are you game?:
Are you willing to do something?
trudge [trʌdʒ] n.
장거리 보행, 도보 여행
connoisseur [kànəsə́ːr, -súər / kɔ̀n-] n.
감정가, 감식가
bouquet [boukéi, buː-] n.
(포도주 등의) 향기
mongrel [mʌ́ŋgrəl, mɑ́ŋ-] n.
잡종개
tremulous [trémjələs] adj.
떨리는, 떠는, 겁많은, 소심한
yelp [jelp] n.
짧고 날카로운 짖음
patter [pǽtər] v.
타닥타닥 걷다(달리다)

forlorn [fəːrlɔ́ːrn] adj.
쓸쓸한, 황량한
blighted [blaitid] adj.
시들은, 망쳐진
ill-omened [-óumənd] adj.
불길한, 불운한

"... I would sooner face a Martini bullet, myself. Are you game for a six-mile trudge, Watson?"

appease [əpíːz] v.
가라앉히다, 진정시키다
swerve [swəːrv] v.
어긋나다, 빗나가다

culpable [kʎlpəbl] adj.
비난할 만한, 과실이 있는

stopped finally in a corner screened by a young beech. Where the two walls joined, several bricks had been loosened, and the crevices left were worn down and rounded upon the lower side, as though they had frequently been used as a ladder. Holmes clambered up, and, taking the dog from me, he dropped it over upon the other side.

"There's the print of wooden-leg's hand," he remarked, as I mounted up beside him. "You see the slight smudge of blood upon the white plaster. What a lucky thing it is that we have had no very heavy rain since yesterday! The scent will lie upon the road in spite of their eight-and-twenty hours' start."

I confess that I had my doubts myself when I reflected upon the great traffic which had passed along the London road in the interval. My fears were soon **appeased**, however. Toby never hesitated or **swerved**, but waddled on in his peculiar rolling fashion. Clearly, the pungent smell of the creosote rose high above all other contending scents.

"Do not imagine," said Holmes, "that I depend for my success in this case upon the mere chance of one of these fellows having put his foot in the chemical. I have knowledge now which would enable me to trace them in many different ways. This, however, is the readiest and, since fortune has put it into our hands, I should be **culpable** if I neglected it. It has, however, prevented the case from becoming the pretty little intellectual problem which it at one time promised to be. There might have been some credit to be gained out of

palpable [pǽlpəbəl] adj.
뚜렷한, 명백한
to spare:
남아돌 만큼의
inexplicable [inéksplikəbəl, ìniksplík-] adj.
설명할 수 없는, 해석할 수 없는

pshaw [ʃɔː] interj.
(초조함, 경멸, 불신 등을 나타내어) 체, 흥, 피
theatrical [θiǽtrik-əl] adj.
연극적인, 과장된
patent [pǽtənt, péit-] adj.
명백한, 확실한
aboveboard [əbʌ́vbɔ̀ːrd] adj.
분명한, 공정한, 정직한
on(in) behalf of~:
~을 대표하여, ~을 위하여
unfulfilled [ʌ̀nfulfíld] adj.
이루지 못한

speculation [spèkjəléiʃ-ən] n.
추측, 추론
sequel [síːkwəl] n.
속편, 이어지는 이야기

it, but for this too **palpable** clue."

"There is credit, and **to spare**," said I. "I assure you, Holmes, that I marvel at the means by which you obtain your results in this case, even more than I did in the Jefferson Hope murder. The thing seems to me to be deeper and more **inexplicable**. How, for example, could you describe with such confidence the wooden-legged man?"

"**Pshaw**, my dear boy! it was simplicity itself. I don't wish to be **theatrical**. It is all **patent** and **above-board**. Two officers who are in command of a convict-guard learn an important secret as to buried treasure. A map is drawn for them by an Englishman named Jonathan Small. You remember that we saw the name upon the chart in Captain Morstan's possession. He had signed it **in behalf of** himself and his associates,—the sign of the four, as he somewhat dramatically called it. Aided by this chart, the officers—or one of them—gets the treasure and brings it to England, leaving, we will suppose, some condition under which he received it **unfulfilled**. Now, then, why did not Jonathan Small get the treasure himself? The answer is obvious. The chart is dated at a time when Morstan was brought into close association with convicts. Jonathan Small did not get the treasure because he and his associates were themselves convicts and could not get away."

"But this is mere **speculation**," said I.

"It is more than that. It is the only hypothesis which covers the facts. Let us see how it fits in with the **sequel**. Major Sholto remains at peace for some years, happy in the possession of his

fright [frait] n.
공포, 두려움

wrong [rɔːŋ, raŋ] v.
피해를 끼치다, 부당하게 대하다

faulty [fɔ́ːlti] adj.
그릇된, 불완전한

"... Now, only one white man's name is on the chart. ..."

regain [rigéin] v.
되찾다, 회복하다

frenzy [frénzi] n.
격분, 광란

lest [lest] conj.
~하지 않게

treasure. Then he receives a letter from India which gives him a great **fright**. What was that?"

"A letter to say that the men whom he had **wronged** had been set free."

"Or had escaped. That is much more likely, for he would have known what their term of imprisonment was. It would not have been a surprise to him. What does he do then? He guards himself against a wooden-legged man,—a white man, mark you, for he mistakes a white tradesman for him, and actually fires a pistol at him. Now, only one white man's name is on the chart. The others are Hindoos or Mohammedans. There is no other white man. Therefore we may say with confidence that the wooden-legged man is identical with Jonathan Small. Does the reasoning strike you as being **faulty**?"

"No: it is clear and concise."

"Well, now, let us put ourselves in the place of Jonathan Small. Let us look at it from his point of view. He comes to England with the double idea of **regaining** what he would consider to be his rights and of having his revenge upon the man who had wronged him. He found out where Sholto lived, and very possibly he established communications with some one inside the house. There is this butler, Lal Rao, whom we have not seen. Mrs. Bernstone gives him far from a good character. Small could not find out, however, where the treasure was hid, for no one ever knew, save the major and one faithful servant who had died. Suddenly Small learns that the major is on his death-bed. In a **frenzy lest** the secret of the treasure die with

run the gauntlet of~:
고난을 당하다, 위험을 감수하다
deter [ditə́:r] v.
단념시키다
memento [miméntou] n.
과거의 기억을 떠올리게 하는 것
should he slay:
if he should slay
whimsical [hwímzik-əl] adj.
변덕스러운, 종작없는, 예측 불허의
bizarre [bizɑ́:r] adj.
기괴한, 별난
follow [fálou / fɔ́lou] v.
이해하다

garret [gǽrət] n.
다락방
confederate [kənfédərit] n.
공범, 공모자
whence [hwens] adv.
어디에서, 어디로부터
a half-pay officer with a damaged *tendo Achillis*:
왓슨을 가리킴
cf. Achilles' tendon, Achilles heel

him, he **runs the gauntlet of** the guards, makes his way to the dying man's window, and is only **deterred** from entering by the presence of his two sons. Mad with hate, however, against the dead man, he enters the room that night, searches his private papers in the hope of discovering some memorandum relating to the treasure, and finally leaves a **memento** of his visit in the short inscription upon the card. He had doubtless planned beforehand that **should he slay** the major he would leave some such record upon the body as a sign that it was not a common murder, but, from the point of view of the four associates, something in the nature of an act of justice. **Whimsical** and **bizarre** conceits of this kind are common enough in the annals of crime, and usually afford valuable indications as to the criminal. Do you **follow** all this?"

"Very clearly."

"Now, what could Jonathan Small do? He could only continue to keep a secret watch upon the efforts made to find the treasure. Possibly he leaves England and only comes back at intervals. Then comes the discovery of the **garret**, and he is instantly informed of it. We again trace the presence of some **confederate** in the household. Jonathan, with his wooden leg, is utterly unable to reach the lofty room of Bartholomew Sholto. He takes with him, however, a rather curious associate, who gets over this difficulty, but dips his naked foot into creosote, **whence** comes Toby, and a six-mile limp for **a half-pay officer** with a damaged *tendo Achillis*."

associate [əsóuʃiit, -èit] n.
동료, 친구, 공범

grudge [grʌʤ] n.
원한, 악의

halter [hɔ́:ltər] n.
교수용 밧줄

decipher [disáifər] v.
풀다, 판독하다,

stride [straid] n.
걸음, 보폭

"But it was the **associate**, and not Jonathan, who committed the crime."

"Quite so. And rather to Jonathan's disgust, to judge by the way he stamped about when he got into the room. He bore no **grudge** against Bartholomew Sholto, and would have preferred if he could have been simply bound and gagged. He did not wish to put his head in a **halter**. There was no help for it, however: the savage instincts of his companion had broken out, and the poison had done its work: so Jonathan Small left his record, lowered the treasure-box to the ground, and followed it himself. That was the train of events as far as I can **decipher** them. Of course as to his personal appearance he must be middle-aged, and must be sunburned after serving his time in such an oven as the Andamans. His height is readily calculated from the length of his **stride**, and we know that he was bearded. His hairiness was the one point which impressed itself upon Thaddeus Sholto when he saw him at the window. I don't know that there is anything else."

"The associate?"

"Ah, well, there is no great mystery in that. But you will know all about it soon enough. How sweet the morning air is! See how that one little cloud floats like a pink feather from some gigantic flamingo. Now the red rim of the sun pushes itself over the London cloud-bank. It shines on a good many folk, but on none, I dare bet, who are on a stranger errand than you and I. How small we feel with our petty ambitions and strivings in the presence of the great elemental forces of nature!

brook [bruk] n.
시내, 개울
perception [pərsépʃən] n.
지각, 이해, 직관

lair [lɛəːr] n.
소굴, 은신처
nasty [nǽsti, náːs-] adj.
고약한, 더러운, 불쾌한

Are you well up in your Jean Paul?"

"Fairly so. I worked back to him through Carlyle."

"That was like following the **brook** to the parent lake. He makes one curious but profound remark. It is that the chief proof of man's real greatness lies in his **perception** of his own smallness. It argues, you see, a power of comparison and of appreciation which is in itself a proof of nobility. There is much food for thought in Richter. You have not a pistol, have you?"

"I have my stick."

"It is just possible that we may need something of the sort if we get to their **lair**. Jonathan I shall leave to you, but if the other turns **nasty** I shall shoot him dead."

He took out his revolver as he spoke, and, having

# 7 The Episode of the Barrel

loaded two of the chambers, he put it back into the right-hand pocket of his jacket.

We had during this time been following the guidance of Toby down the half-**rural** villa-lined roads which lead to the metropolis. Now, however, we were beginning to come among continuous streets, where laborers and dockmen were already **astir**, and slatternly women were taking down shutters and brushing door-steps. At the square-topped corner public houses business was just beginning, and rough-looking men were emerging, rubbing their sleeves across their beards after their morning wet. Strange dogs **sauntered** up and stared wonderingly at us as we passed, but our **inimitable** Toby looked neither to the right nor to the left, but trotted onwards with his nose to the ground and an occasional eager whine which spoke of a hot scent.

We had traversed Streatham, Brixton, Camberwell, and now found ourselves in Kennington Lane, having borne away through the side-streets to the east of the Oval. The men whom we pursued seemed to have taken a curiously zigzag road, with the idea probably of escaping observation. They had never kept to the main road if a parallel side-street would serve their turn. At the foot of Kennington Lane they had edged away to the left through Bond Street and Miles Street. Where the latter street turns into Knight's Place, Toby ceased to advance, but began to run backwards and forwards with one ear cocked and the other drooping, the very picture of **canine indecision**. Then he **waddled** round in circles, looking up to us from

---

rural [rú-ərəl] adj.
시골의, 지방의
astir [əstə́:r] adj.
움직여, 활동하여
saunter [sɔ́:ntə:r, sά:n-] v.
어슬렁거리며 걷다
inimitable [inímitəbəl] adj.
비길 데 없는, 모방할 수 없는

canine [kéinain, kǽn-] adj.
개의, 개와 관련된
indecision [ìndisíʒən] n.
우유부단, 망설임
waddle [wάdl / wɔ́dl] v.
아장아장 걷다

growl [graul] v.
으르렁거리다

tug [tʌg] v.
세게 잡아당기다
leash [liːʃ] n.
밧줄

sawyer [sɔ́ːjəːr] n.
톱질하는 인부
triumphant [traiʌ́mfənt] adj.
성공한, 의기양양한
cask [kæsk, kɑːsk] n.
통

time to time, as if to ask for sympathy in his embarrassment.

"What the deuce is the matter with the dog?" **growled** Holmes. "They surely would not take a cab, or go off in a balloon."

"Perhaps they stood here for some time," I suggested.

"Ah! it's all right. He's off again," said my companion, in a tone of relief.

He was indeed off, for after sniffing round again he suddenly made up his mind, and darted away with an energy and determination such as he had not yet shown. The scent appeared to be much hotter than before, for he had not even to put his nose on the ground, but **tugged** at his **leash** and tried to break into a run. I could see by the gleam in Holmes's eyes that he thought we were nearing the end of our journey.

Our course now ran down Nine Elms until we came to Broderick and Nelson's large timber-yard, just past the White Eagle tavern. Here the dog, frantic with excitement, turned down through the side-gate into the enclosure, where the **sawyers** were already at work. On the dog raced through sawdust and shavings, down an alley, round a passage, between two wood-piles, and finally, with a **triumphant** yelp, sprang upon a large barrel which still stood upon the hand-trolley on which it had been brought. With lolling tongue and blinking eyes, Toby stood upon the **cask**, looking from one to the other of us for some sign of appreciation. The staves of the barrel and the wheels of the trolley were smeared with a dark liquid, and the whole air was heavy with the smell of creosote.

Sherlock Holmes and I looked blankly at each other, and then burst simultaneously into an uncontrollable fit of laughter.

# 8 The Baker Street Irregulars

infallibility [ìnfæ̀ləbíləti] n.
절대 확실함
cart [kɑːrt] v.
짐차(수레)로 나르다

"What now?" I asked. "Toby has lost his character for **infallibility**."

"He acted according to his lights," said Holmes, lifting him down from the barrel and walking him out of the timber-yard. "If you consider how much creosote is **carted** about London in one day, it is no great wonder that our trail should have been crossed. It is much used now, especially for the seasoning of wood. Poor Toby is not to blame."

"We must get on the main scent again, I suppose."

"Yes. And, fortunately, we have no distance to go. Evidently what puzzled the dog at the corner of Knight's Place was that there were two different trails running in opposite directions. We took the wrong one. It only remains to follow the other."

There was no difficulty about this. On leading Toby to the place where he had committed his fault, he cast about in a wide circle and finally dashed off in a fresh direction.

"We must take care that he does not now bring us to the place where the creosote-barrel came from," I observed.

"I had thought of that. But you notice that he keeps on the pavement, whereas the barrel passed down the roadway. No, we are on the true scent now."

It tended down towards the river-side, running through Belmont Place and Prince's Street. At the end of Broad Street it ran right down to the water's edge, where there was a small wooden **wharf**. Toby led us to the very edge of this, and there stood whining, looking out on the dark current beyond.

"We are out of luck," said Holmes. "They have taken to a boat here."

Several small punts and skiffs were lying about in the water and on the edge of the wharf. We took Toby round to each in turn, but, though he sniffed earnestly, he made no sign.

Close to the **rude landing-stage** was a small brick house, with a wooden placard **slung** out through the second window. "Mordecai Smith" was printed across it in large letters, and, underneath, "Boats to hire by the hour or day." A second inscription above the door informed us that a steam **launch** was kept,—a statement which was confirmed by a great pile of coke upon the **jetty**. Sherlock Holmes looked slowly round, and his face assumed an **ominous** expression.

wharf [hwɔːrf] n.
부두

rude [ruːd] adj.
허름한, 조잡한
landing stage:
부잔교 浮棧橋; 물건 등을 옮기기 위해 선박과 육지를 연결하는 평평한 구조물
sling [slɪŋ] v.
메다, 걸다
launch [lɔːntʃ, lɑːntʃ] n.
노 엔진을 사용하는 대형 보트, 소증기선
jetty [dʒéti] n.
부두, 방파제
ominous [ámənəs / ɔ́m-] adj.
불길한

preconcerted [prìːkənsə́ːrtid] adj. 사전에 준비된

imp [imp] n. 개구쟁이

prodigy [prádədʒi / prɔ́d-] n. 신동 神童

forward [fɔ́ːrwərd] adj. 주제넘은, 조숙한

"This looks bad," said he. "These fellows are sharper than I expected. They seem to have covered their tracks. There has, I fear, been **preconcerted** management here."

He was approaching the door of the house, when it opened, and a little, curly-headed lad of six came running out, followed by a stoutish, red-faced woman with a large sponge in her hand.

"You come back and be washed, Jack," she shouted. "Come back, you young **imp**; for if your father comes home and finds you like that, he'll let us hear of it."

"Dear little chap!" said Holmes, strategically. "What a rosy-cheeked young rascal! Now, Jack, is there anything you would like?"

The youth pondered for a moment. "I'd like a shillin'," said he.

"Nothing you would like better?"

"I'd like two shillin' better," the **prodigy** answered, after some thought.

"Here you are, then! Catch!—A fine child, Mrs. Smith!"

"Lor' bless you, sir, he is that, and **forward**. He gets a'most too much for me to manage, 'specially when my man is away days at a time."

"Away, is he?" said Holmes, in a disappointed voice. "I am sorry for that, for I wanted to speak to Mr. Smith."

"He's been away since yesterday mornin', sir, and, truth to tell, I am beginnin' to feel frightened about him. But if it was about a boat, sir, maybe I could serve as well."

"I wanted to hire his steam launch."

"Why, bless you, sir, it is in the steam launch that he has gone. That's what puzzles me; for I know there ain't more coals in her than would take her to about Woolwich and back. If he'd been away in the barge I'd ha' thought nothin'; for many a time a job has taken him as far as Gravesend, and then if there was much doin' there he might ha' stayed over. But what good is a steam launch without coals?"

"He might have bought some at a wharf down the river."

"He might, sir, but it weren't his way. Many a time I've heard him call out at the prices they charge for a few odd bags. Besides, I don't like that wooden-legged man, wi' his ugly face and **outlandish** talk. What did he want always knockin'

---

outlandish [autlǽndiʃ] adj.
이국풍의, 기이한, 희한한

"I'd like two shillin' better,"

about here for?"

"A wooden-legged man?" said Holmes, with bland surprise.

"Yes, sir, a brown, monkey-faced chap that's called more'n once for my old man. It was him that roused him up yesternight, and, what's more, my man knew he was comin', for he had steam up in the launch. I tell you straight, sir, I don't feel easy in my mind about it."

"But, my dear Mrs. Smith," said Holmes, shrugging his shoulders, "You are frightening yourself about nothing. How could you possibly tell that it was the wooden-legged man who came in the night? I don't quite understand how you can be so sure."

"His voice, sir. I knew his voice, which is kind o' thick and foggy. He tapped at the winder,—about three it would be. 'Show a leg, matey,' says he: 'time to turn out guard.' My old man woke up Jim,—that's my eldest,—and away they went, without so much as a word to me. I could hear the wooden leg **clackin**' on the stones."

"And was this wooden-legged man alone?"

"Couldn't say, I am sure, sir. I didn't hear no one else."

"I am sorry, Mrs. Smith, for I wanted a steam launch, and I have heard good reports of the—Let me see, what is her name?"

"The *Aurora*, sir."

"Ah! She's not that old green launch with a yellow line, very broad in the beam?"

"No, indeed. She's as trim a little thing as any on the river. She's been fresh painted, black with two red streaks."

---

clack [klæk] v.
철컥 소리내다

> wherry [hwéri] n.
> 나룻배, 거룻배, 어선

> under protest:
> 마지못해, 이의를 제기하면서

> colossal [kəlásəl / -lɔ́sl] adj.
> 막대한, 거대한
> labyrinth [lǽbərìnθ] n.
> 미로

"Thanks. I hope that you will hear soon from Mr. Smith. I am going down the river; and if I should see anything of the *Aurora* I shall let him know that you are uneasy. A black funnel, you say?"

"No, sir. Black with a white band."

"Ah, of course. It was the sides which were black. Good-morning, Mrs. Smith.—There is a boatman here with a **wherry**, Watson. We shall take it and cross the river.

"The main thing with people of that sort," said Holmes, as we sat in the sheets of the wherry, "is never to let them think that their information can be of the slightest importance to you. If you do, they will instantly shut up like an oyster. If you listen to them **under protest**, as it were, you are very likely to get what you want."

"Our course now seems pretty clear," said I.

"What would you do, then?"

"I would engage a launch and go down the river on the track of the *Aurora*."

"My dear fellow, it would be a **colossal** task. She may have touched at any wharf on either side of the stream between here and Greenwich. Below the bridge there is a perfect **labyrinth** of landing-places for miles. It would take you days and days to exhaust them, if you set about it alone."

"Employ the police, then."

"No. I shall probably call Athelney Jones in at the last moment. He is not a bad fellow, and I should not like to do anything which would injure him professionally. But I have a fancy for working it out myself, now that we have gone so far."

"Could we advertise, then, asking for information

wharfinger [hwɔ́:rfindʒəːr] n.
부두관리인
runaway [rʌ́nəwèi] n.
도망자, 탈주자

afoot [əfút] adj.
움직이는, 도보로

from **wharfingers**?"

"Worse and worse! Our men would know that the chase was hot at their heels, and they would be off out of the country. As it is, they are likely enough to leave, but as long as they think they are perfectly safe they will be in no hurry. Jones's energy will be of use to us there, for his view of the case is sure to push itself into the daily Press, and the **runaways** will think that every one is off on the wrong scent."

"What are we to do, then?" I asked, as we landed near Millbank Penitentiary.

"Take this hansom, drive home, have some breakfast, and get an hour's sleep. It is quite on the cards that we may be **afoot** to-night again. Stop at a telegraph-office, cabby! We will keep Toby, for he may be of use to us yet."

We pulled up at the Great Peter Street post-office, and Holmes despatched his wire.

"Whom do you think that is to?" he asked, as we resumed our journey.

"I am sure I don't know."

"You remember the Baker Street division of the detective police force whom I employed in the Jefferson Hope case?"

"Well," said I, laughing.

"This is just the case where they might be invaluable. If they fail, I have other resources; but I shall try them first. That wire was to my dirty little lieutenant, Wiggins, and I expect that he and his gang will be with us before we have finished our breakfast."

It was between eight and nine o'clock now, and

limp [limp] adj.
기력없는
befog [bifǽg, -fɔ́(:)g] v.
어리둥절하게 하다
antipathy [æntípəθi] n.
반감, 혐오
petty [péti] adj.
사소한, 하찮은, 이차적인
tenfold [ténfòuld, -´-] adj.
10배의, 10겹의

ubiquitous [ju:bíkwətəs] adj.
도처에 존재하는

I was conscious of a strong reaction after the successive excitements of the night. I was **limp** and weary, **befogged** in mind and fatigued in body. I had not the professional enthusiasm which carried my companion on, nor could I look at the matter as a mere abstract intellectual problem. As far as the death of Bartholomew Sholto went, I had heard little good of him, and could feel no intense **antipathy** to his murderers. The treasure, however, was a different matter. That, or part of it, belonged rightfully to Miss Morstan. While there was a chance of recovering it I was ready to devote my life to the one object. True, if I found it it would probably put her forever beyond my reach. Yet it would be a **petty** and selfish love which would be influenced by such a thought as that. If Holmes could work to find the criminals, I had a **tenfold** stronger reason to urge me on to find the treasure.

A bath at Baker Street and a complete change freshened me up wonderfully. When I came down to our room I found the breakfast laid and Homes pouring out the coffee.

"Here it is," said he, laughing, and pointing to an open newspaper.

"The energetic Jones and the **ubiquitous** reporter have fixed it up between them. But you have had enough of the case. Better have your ham and eggs first."

I took the paper from him and read the short notice, which was headed "Mysterious Business at Upper Norwood."

foul play:
부정 행위, 배신 행위, 폭행
gem [dʒem] n.
보석, 주옥, 일품
inherit [inhérit] v.
물려받다, 상속하다
gratifying [grǽtəfàiiŋ] adj.
흡족한, 유쾌한
miscreant [mískriənt] n.
악한

About twelve o'clock last night [said the *Standard*] Mr. Bartholomew Sholto, of Pondicherry Lodge, Upper Norwood, was found dead in his room under circumstances which point to **foul play**. As far as we can learn, no actual traces of violence were found upon Mr. Sholto's person, but a valuable collection of Indian **gems** which the deceased gentleman had **inherited** from his father has been carried off. The discovery was first made by Mr. Sherlock Holmes and Dr. Watson, who had called at the house with Mr. Thaddeus Sholto, brother of the deceased. By a singular piece of good fortune, Mr. Athelney Jones, the well-known member of the detective police force, happened to be at the Norwood Police Station, and was on the ground within half an hour of the first alarm. His trained and experienced faculties were at once directed towards the detection of the criminals, with the **gratifying** result that the brother, Thaddeus Sholto, has already been arrested, together with the housekeeper, Mrs. Bernstone, an Indian butler named Lal Rao, and a porter, or gatekeeper, named McMurdo. It is quite certain that the thief or thieves were well acquainted with the house, for Mr. Jones's well-known technical knowledge and his powers of minute observation have enabled him to prove conclusively that the **miscreants** could not have entered by the door or by the window, but must have made their way across the roof of the building, and so through a trap-door into a room which communicated with that in which the body was found. This

haphazard [hǽphǽzərd] adj.
되는대로의, 무작정의

a close shave:
위기일발, 구사일생

wail [weil] n.
울부짖음, 통곡, 구슬픈 소리
expostulation [ikspástʃulèiʃən/-pós-] n.
훈계, 반대

irregular [irégjələr] n.
(military) (게릴라 등) 비정규병
street Arab:
부랑아, 방랑자, 정처없는 사람
tumultuous [tju:mʌltʃuəs] adj.
떠들썩한, 소란스런

fact, which has been very clearly made out, proves conclusively that it was no mere **haphazard** burglary. The prompt and energetic action of the officers of the law shows the great advantage of the presence on such occasions of a single vigorous and masterful mind. We cannot but think that it supplies an argument to those who would wish to see our detectives more decentralized, and so brought into closer and more effective touch with the cases which it is their duty to investigate."

"Isn't it gorgeous!" said Holmes, grinning over his coffee-cup. "What do you think of it?"

"I think that we have had a **close shave** ourselves of being arrested for the crime."

"So do I. I wouldn't answer for our safety now, if he should happen to have another of his attacks of energy."

At this moment there was a loud ring at the bell, and I could hear Mrs. Hudson, our landlady, raising her voice in a **wail** of **expostulation** and dismay.

"By heaven, Holmes," I said, half rising, "I believe that they are really after us."

"No, it's not quite so bad as that. It is the unofficial force,—the Baker Street **irregulars**."

As he spoke, there came a swift pattering of naked feet upon the stairs, a clatter of high voices, and in rushed a dozen dirty and ragged little **street-Arabs**. There was some show of discipline among them, despite their **tumultuous** entry, for they instantly drew up in line and stood facing us with expectant faces. One of their number, taller

scarecrow [skéərkròu] n.
초라한 사람

three bob and a tanner: (slang) three shillings and six pence

whereabout [hwé-ərəbàuts] n.
소재, 위치, 거처

and older than the others, stood forward with an air of lounging superiority which was very funny in such a disreputable little **scarecrow**.

"Got your message, sir," said he, "and brought 'em on sharp. **Three bob and a tanner** for tickets."

"Here you are," said Holmes, producing some silver. "In future they can report to you, Wiggins, and you to me. I cannot have the house invaded in this way. However, it is just as well that you should all hear the instructions. I want to find the **whereabouts** of a steam launch called the *Aurora*, owner Mordecai Smith, black with two red streaks, funnel black with a white band. She is down the river somewhere. I want one boy to be at Mordecai Smith's landing-stage opposite Millbank to say if the boat comes back. You must divide it

out among yourselves, and do both banks thoroughly. Let me know the moment you have news. Is that all clear?"

"Yes, **guv'nor**," said Wiggins.

"The old scale of pay, and a guinea to the boy who finds the boat. Here's a day in advance. Now off you go!"

He handed them a shilling each, and away they buzzed down the stairs, and I saw them a moment later streaming down the street.

"If the launch is above water they will find her," said Holmes, as he rose from the table and lit his pipe. "They can go everywhere, see everything, **overhear** every one. I expect to hear before evening that they have spotted her. In the mean while, we can do nothing but await results. We cannot pick up the broken trail until we find either the *Aurora* or Mr. Mordecai Smith."

"Toby could eat these scraps, I dare say. Are you going to bed, Holmes?"

"No: I am not tired. I have a curious **constitution**. I never remember feeling tired by work, though idleness exhausts me completely. I am going to smoke and to think over this queer business to which my fair client has introduced us. If ever man had an easy task, this of ours ought to be. Wooden-legged men are not so common, but the other man must, I should think, be absolutely unique."

"That other man again!"

"I have no wish to make a mystery of him to you, anyway. But you must have formed your own opinion. Now, do consider the data. **Diminutive**

fetter [fétər] v.
차꼬(족쇄)를 채우다, 속박하다, 구속하다

mace [meis] n.
전곤 戰棍; 머리에 큰 못이 박힌 곤봉 모양의 중세무기

agility [ədʒíləti] n.
민첩함

proper [prápər / próp-] adj.
진정한, 엄밀한 의미의

thong [θɔ(:)ŋ, θαŋ] n.
엄지와 두 번째 발가락 사이를 지니는 끈을 가진 샌들

blowpipe [blóupàip] n.
바람총

gazetteer [gæzətíər] n.
지명사전

aborigine [æbərídʒəni:] n.
원주민

anthropologist
[ænθərəpáləjʒist / -pól-] n.
인류학자

footmarks, toes never **fettered** by boots, naked feet, stone-headed wooden **mace**, great **agility**, small poisoned darts. What do you make of all this?"

"A savage!" I exclaimed. "Perhaps one of those Indians who were the associates of Jonathan Small."

"Hardly that," said he. "When first I saw signs of strange weapons I was inclined to think so; but the remarkable character of the footmarks caused me to reconsider my views. Some of the inhabitants of the Indian Peninsula are small men, but none could have left such marks as that. The Hindoo **proper** has long and thin feet. The sandal-wearing Mohammedan has the great toe well separated from the others, because the **thong** is commonly passed between. These little darts, too, could only be shot in one way. They are from a **blow-pipe**. Now, then, where are we to find our savage?"

"South American," I hazarded.

He stretched his hand up, and took down a bulky volume from the shelf.

"This is the first volume of a **gazetteer** which is now being published. It may be looked upon as the very latest authority. What have we here? 'Andaman Islands, situated 340 miles to the north of Sumatra, in the Bay of Bengal.' Hum! hum! What's all this? Moist climate, coral reefs, sharks, Port Blair, convict-barracks, Rutland Island, cottonwoods—Ah, here we are. 'The **aborigines** of the Andaman Islands may perhaps claim the distinction of being the smallest race upon this earth, though some **anthropologists** prefer the Bushmen of Africa, the Digger Indians of America, and the Terra del Fuegians. The average height is rather

morose [məróus] adj.
시무룩한, 까다로운
intractable [intrǽktəbəl] adj.
다루기 힘든, 고집센
mark [mɑːrk] v.
주목하다, 유의하다
hideous [hídiəs] adj.
무서운, 몹시 추한, 극악 무도한
misshapen [misʃéipən] adj.
보기 흉한, 기형의
massacre [mǽsəkəːr] n.
대학살
leave to (one's) own devices:
좋도록 내버려두다
unaided [ʌnéidid] adj.
도움이 없는, 독립의
ghastly [gǽstli / gáːst-] adj.
창백한, 무시무시한

islander [áiləndər] n.
섬사람
in time:
장차, 조만간
regularly [régjələːrli] adv.
완전하게, 철저히

air [ɛər] n.
멜로디, 선율

below four feet, although many full-grown adults may be found who are very much smaller than this. They are a fierce, **morose**, and **intractable** people, though capable of forming most devoted friendships when their confidence has once been gained.' **Mark** that, Watson. Now, then, listen to this. 'They are naturally **hideous**, having large, **misshapen** heads, small, fierce eyes, and distorted features. Their feet and hands, however, are remarkably small. So intractable and fierce are they that all the efforts of the British officials have failed to win them over in any degree. They have always been a terror to shipwrecked crews, braining the survivors with their stone-headed clubs, or shooting them with their poisoned arrows. These **massacres** are invariably concluded by a cannibal feast.' Nice, amiable people, Watson! If this fellow had been **left to his own unaided devices** this affair might have taken an even more **ghastly** turn. I fancy that, even as it is, Jonathan Small would give a good deal not to have employed him."

"But how came he to have so singular a companion?"

"Ah, that is more than I can tell. Since, however, we had already determined that Small had come from the Andamans, it is not so very wonderful that this **islander** should be with him. No doubt we shall know all about it **in time**. Look here, Watson; you look **regularly** done. Lie down there on the sofa, and see if I can put you to sleep."

He took up his violin from the corner, and as I stretched myself out he began to play some low, dreamy, melodious **air**,—his own, no doubt, for

improvisation [ìmprɑ̀vəzéiʃən, ìmprəvi-] n.
즉흥연주

gaunt [gɔ:nt] adj.
여윈, 수척한

he had a remarkable gift for **improvisation**. I have a vague remembrance of his **gaunt** limbs, his earnest face, and the rise and fall of his bow. Then I seemed to be floated peacefully away upon a soft sea of sound, until I found myself in dreamland, with the sweet face of Mary Morstan looking down upon me.

## 9 A Break in the Chain

It was late in the afternoon before I woke, strengthened and refreshed. Sherlock Holmes still sat exactly as I had left him, save that he had laid aside his violin and was deep in a book. He looked across at me, as I stirred, and I noticed that his face was dark and troubled.

"You have slept soundly," he said. "I feared that our talk would wake you."

"I heard nothing," I answered. "Have you had fresh news, then?"

"Unfortunately, no. I confess that I am surprised and disappointed. I expected something definite by this time. Wiggins has just been up to report. He says that no trace can be found of the launch. It is a provoking check, for every hour is of importance."

"Can I do anything? I am perfectly fresh now,

and quite ready for another night's outing."

"No, we can do nothing. We can only wait. If we go ourselves, the message might come in our absence, and delay be caused. You can do what you will, but I must remain on guard."

"Then I shall run over to Camberwell and call upon Mrs. Cecil Forrester. She asked me to, yesterday."

"On Mrs. Cecil Forrester?" asked Holmes, with the twinkle of a smile in his eyes.

"Well, of course Miss Morstan too. They were anxious to hear what happened."

"I would not tell them too much," said Holmes. "Women are never to be entirely trusted—not the best of them."

I did not pause to argue over this **atrocious** sentiment.

"I shall be back in an hour or two," I remarked.

"All right! Good luck! But, I say, if you are crossing the water you may as well return Toby, for I don't think it is at all likely that we shall have any use for him now."

I took our mongrel accordingly, and left him, together with a half-sovereign, at the old naturalist's in Pinchin Lane. At Camberwell I found Miss Morstan a little weary after her night's adventures, but very eager to hear the news. Mrs. Forrester, too, was full of curiosity. I told them all that we had done, suppressing, however, the more dreadful parts of the tragedy. Thus, although I spoke of Mr. Sholto's death, I said nothing of the exact manner and method of it. With all my omissions, however, there was enough to startle and amaze them.

---

atrocious [ətróuʃəs] adj.
지나친, 매우 심한

## 9 A Break in the Chain

ruffian [rʌ́fiən, -fjən] n.
불한당, 악한
earl [əːrl] n.
백작

knight-errant [-́érənt] n.
편력하는 기사

elation [iléiʃən] n.
기쁨, 의기양양함

unfounded [ʌnfáundid] adj.
근거 없는, 사실 무근의

"It is a romance!" cried Mrs. Forrester. "An injured lady, half a million in treasure, a black cannibal, and a wooden-legged **ruffian**. They take the place of the conventional dragon or wicked **earl**."

"And two **knight-errants** to the rescue," added Miss Morstan, with a bright glance at me.

"Why, Mary, your fortune depends upon the issue of this search. I don't think that you are nearly excited enough. Just imagine what it must be to be so rich, and to have the world at your feet!"

It sent a little thrill of joy to my heart to notice that she showed no sign of **elation** at the prospect. On the contrary, she gave a toss of her proud head, as though the matter were one in which she took small interest.

"It is for Mr. Thaddeus Sholto that I am anxious," she said. "Nothing else is of any consequence; but I think that he has behaved most kindly and honorably throughout. It is our duty to clear him of this dreadful and **unfounded** charge."

It was evening before I left Camberwell, and quite dark by the time I reached home. My companion's book and pipe lay by his chair, but he had disappeared. I looked about in the hope of seeing a note, but there was none.

"I suppose that Mr. Sherlock Holmes has gone out," I said to Mrs. Hudson as she came up to lower the blinds.

"No, sir. He has gone to his room, sir. Do you know, sir," sinking her voice into an impressive whisper, "I am afraid for his health?"

"Why so, Mrs. Hudson?"

"Well, he's that strange, sir. After you was gone

he walked and he walked, up and down, and up and down, until I was weary of the sound of his footstep. Then I heard him talking to himself and muttering, and every time the bell rang out he came on the stairhead, with 'What is that, Mrs. Hudson?' And now he has slammed off to his room, but I can hear him walking away the same as ever. I hope he's not going to be ill, sir. I **ventured** to say something to him about cooling medicine, but he turned on me, sir, with such a look that I don't know how ever I got out of the room."

"I don't think that you have any cause to be uneasy, Mrs. Hudson," I answered. "I have seen him like this before. He has some small matter upon his mind which makes him restless."

I tried to speak lightly to our **worthy** landlady, but I was myself somewhat uneasy when through the long night I still from time to time heard the dull sound of his **tread**, and knew how his keen spirit was **chafing** against this involuntary inaction.

At breakfast-time he looked worn and haggard, with a little fleck of feverish color upon either cheek.

"You are knocking yourself up, old man," I remarked. "I heard you marching about in the night."

"No, I could not sleep," he answered. "This **infernal** problem is consuming me. It is too much to be **balked** by so petty an obstacle, when all else had been overcome. I know the men, the launch, everything; and yet I can get no news. I have set other agencies at work, and used every means **at my disposal**. The whole river has been searched

## 9 A Break in the Chain

on either side, but there is no news, nor has Mrs. Smith heard of her husband. I shall come to the conclusion soon that they have **scuttled** the craft. But there are objections to that."

"Or that Mrs. Smith has put us on a wrong scent."

"No, I think that may be **dismissed**. I had inquiries made, and there is a launch of that description."

"Could it have gone up the river?"

"I have considered that possibility too, and there is a search-party who will work up as far as Richmond. If no news comes to-day, I shall start off myself to-morrow, and go for the men rather than the boat. But surely, surely, we shall hear something."

We did not, however. Not a word came to us either from Wiggins or from the other agencies. There were articles in most of the papers upon the Norwood tragedy. They all appeared to be rather **hostile** to the unfortunate Thaddeus Sholto. No fresh details were to be found, however, in any of them, **save** that an **inquest** was to be held upon the following day. I walked over to Camberwell in the evening to report our ill success to the ladies, and on my return I found Holmes **dejected** and somewhat **morose**. He would hardly reply to my questions, and busied himself all the evening in an **abstruse** chemical analysis which involved much heating of retorts and distilling of vapors, ending at last in a smell which fairly drove me out of the apartment. Up to the **small hours** of the morning I could hear the clinking of his test-tubes which told me that he was still engaged in his **malodorous** experiment.

start [stɑːrt] n.
흠칫 놀람

loath, loth [louθ] adj.
싫은, 꺼림칙한
despondent [dispɑ́ndənt / -spɔ́nd-] adj.
낙심한, 풀이 죽은

In the early dawn I woke with a **start**, and was surprised to find him standing by my bedside, clad in a rude sailor dress with a pea-jacket, and a coarse red scarf round his neck.

"I am off down the river, Watson," said he. "I have been turning it over in my mind, and I can see only one way out of it. It is worth trying, at all events."

"Surely I can come with you, then?" said I.

"No; you can be much more useful if you will remain here as my representative. I am **loth** to go, for it is quite on the cards that some message may come during the day, though Wiggins was **despondent** about it last night. I want you to open all notes and telegrams, and to act on your own judgment if any news should come. Can I rely

## 9 A Break in the Chain

upon you?"

"Most certainly."

"I am afraid that you will not be able to wire to me, for I can hardly tell yet where I may find myself. If I am in luck, however, I may not be gone so very long. I shall have news of some sort or other before I get back."

I had heard nothing of him by breakfast-time. On opening the *Standard*, however, I found that there was a fresh allusion to the business.

With reference to the Upper Norwood tragedy [it remarked], we have reason to believe that the matter promises to be even more complex and mysterious than was originally supposed. Fresh evidence has shown that it is quite impossible that Mr. Thaddeus Sholto could have been in any way concerned in the matter. He and the housekeeper, Mrs. Bernstone, were both released yesterday evening. It is believed, however, that the police have a clue as to the real **culprits**, and that it is being prosecuted by Mr. Athelney Jones, of **Scotland Yard**, with all his well-known energy and **sagacity**. Further arrests may be expected at any moment.

"That is satisfactory so far as it goes," thought I. "Friend Sholto is safe, at any rate. I wonder what the fresh clue may be, though it seems to be a stereotyped form whenever the police have made a **blunder**."

I tossed the paper down upon the table, but at that moment my eye caught an advertisement in the **agony column**. It ran in this way:

Lost.—Whereas Mordecai Smith, boatman, and his son, Jim, left Smith's Wharf at or about three o'clock last Tuesday morning in the steam launch *Aurora*, black with two red stripes, funnel black with a white band, the sum of five pounds will be paid to anyone who can give information to Mrs. Smith, at Smith's Wharf, or at 221b Baker Street, **as to** the whereabouts of the **said** Mordecai Smith and the launch *Aurora*."

This was clearly Holmes's doing. The Baker Street address was enough to prove that. It struck me as rather **ingenious**, because it might be read by the **fugitives** without their seeing in it more than the natural anxiety of a wife for her missing husband.

It was a long day. Every time that a knock came to the door, or a sharp step passed in the street, I imagined that it was either Holmes returning or an answer to his advertisement. I tried to read, but my thoughts would wander off to our strange **quest** and to the **ill-assorted** and **villainous** pair whom we were pursuing. Could there be, I wondered, some radical flaw in my companion's reasoning. Might he not be suffering from some huge **self-deception**? Was it not possible that his **nimble** and speculative mind had built up this wild theory upon faulty **premises**? I had never known him to be wrong; and yet the keenest reasoner may occasionally be deceived. He was likely, I thought, to fall into error through the over-refinement of

bizarre [bizá:r] adj.
기괴한, 별난
tend [tend] v.
~하는 경향이 있다, ~로 향하다
outré [u:tréi] adj.
(French) 기이한, 이상한

brusque [brʌsk / brusk] adj.
무뚝뚝한, 퉁명스러운
masterful [mǽstə:rfəl, má:s-] adj. 오만한, 주인티를 내는
downcast [ˈkæst / ˈkɑ̀:st] adj.
의기 소침한, 고개를 숙인

mop [mɑp / mɔp] v.
닦다, (물, 땀 등을) 훔치다
bandanna [bændǽnə] n.
큰 손수건, 밴대나

his logic,—his preference for a subtle and **bizarre** explanation when a plainer and more commonplace one lay ready to his hand. Yet, on the other hand, I had myself seen the evidence, and I had heard the reasons for his deductions. When I looked back on the long chain of curious circumstances, many of them trivial in themselves, but all **tending** in the same direction, I could not disguise from myself that even if Holmes's explanation were incorrect the true theory must be equally **outré** and startling.

At three o'clock in the afternoon there was a loud peal at the bell, an authoritative voice in the hall, and, to my surprise, no less a person than Mr. Athelney Jones was shown up to me. Very different was he, however, from the **brusque** and **masterful** professor of common sense who had taken over the case so confidently at Upper Norwood. His expression was **downcast**, and his bearing meek and even apologetic.

"Good-day, sir; good-day," said he. "Mr. Sherlock Holmes is out, I understand."

"Yes, and I cannot be sure when he will be back. But perhaps you would care to wait. Take that chair and try one of these cigars."

"Thank you; I don't mind if I do," said he, **mopping** his face with a red **bandanna** handkerchief.

"And a whiskey-and-soda?"

"Well, half a glass. It is very hot for the time of year; and I have had a good deal to worry and try me. You know my theory about this Norwood case?"

"I remember that you expressed one."

"Well, I have been obliged to reconsider it. I had my net drawn tightly round Mr. Sholto, sir,

alibi [ǽləbài] n.
현장 부재(증명), 알리바이, 구실, 변명
at stake: 위기에 처한

promising [prámǝsiŋ / prɔ́m-]
adj. 유망한, 믿음직한
wire [waiǝ:r] n.
전보, 전신
clue [klu:] n.
실마리, 단서

throw off:
잘못된 방향으로 이끌다, 속이다

when pop he went through a hole in the middle of it. He was able to prove an **alibi** which could not be shaken. From the time that he left his brother's room he was never out of sight of someone or other. So it could not be he who climbed over roofs and through trap-doors. It's a very dark case, and my professional credit is **at stake**. I should be very glad of a little assistance."

"We all need help sometimes," said I.

"Your friend Mr. Sherlock Holmes is a wonderful man, sir," said he, in a husky and confidential voice. "He's a man who is not to be beat. I have known that young man go into a good many cases, but I never saw the case yet that he could not throw a light upon. He is irregular in his methods, and a little quick perhaps in jumping at theories; but, on the whole, I think he would have made a most **promising** officer and I don't care who knows it. I have had a **wire** from him this morning, by which I understand that he has got some **clue** to this Sholto business. Here is his message."

He took the telegram out of his pocket, and handed it to me. It was dated from Poplar at twelve o'clock. "Go to Baker Street at once," it said. "If I have not returned, wait for me. I am close on the track of the Sholto gang. You can come with us to-night if you want to be in at the finish."

"This sounds well. He has evidently picked up the scent again," said I.

"Ah, then he has been at fault too," exclaimed Jones, with evident satisfaction. "Even the best of us are **thrown off** sometimes. Of course this may prove to be a false alarm; but it is my duty as an

## 9 A Break in the Chain

officer of the law to allow no chance to slip. But there is some one at the door. Perhaps this is he."

A heavy step was heard ascending the stair, with a great **wheezing** and rattling as from a man who was sorely put to it for breath. Once or twice he stopped, as though the climb were too much for him, but at last he made his way to our door and entered. His appearance corresponded to the sounds which we had heard. He was an aged man, clad in **seafaring garb**, with an old pea-jacket buttoned up to his throat. His back was bowed, his knees were shaky, and his breathing was painfully **asthmatic**. As he leaned upon a thick oaken **cudgel** his shoulders heaved in the effort to draw the air into his lungs. He had a colored scarf round his chin, and I could see little of his face **save** a pair of keen dark eyes, overhung by bushy white brows, and long gray side-whiskers. Altogether he gave me the impression of a respectable master mariner who had fallen into years and poverty.

"What is it, my man?" I asked.

He looked about him in the slow methodical fashion of old age.

"Is Mr. Sherlock Holmes here?" said he.

"No; but I am **acting** for him. You can tell me any message you have for him."

"It was to him himself I was to tell it," said he.

"But I tell you I am acting for him. Was it about Mordecai Smith's boat?"

"Yes. I knows well where it is. An' I knows where the men he is after are. An' I knows where the treasure is. I knows all about it."

"Then tell me, and I shall let him know."

petulant [pétʃələnt] adj.
성마른, 언짢은
obstinacy [ábstənəsi / ɔ́b-] n.
완고함, 고집셈
ain't: am not

pretty [príti] adj.
상당히 나쁜, 끔찍한, 형편없는

none the worse:
전혀 손해보지 않는, 전혀 나빠지지 않는
recompense [rékəmpèns] v.
보상하다

"It was to him I was to tell it," he repeated, with the **petulant obstinacy** of a very old man.

"Well, you must wait for him."

"No, no; I **ain't** goin' to lose a whole day to please no one. If Mr. Holmes ain't here, then Mr. Holmes must find it all out for himself. I don't care about the look of either of you, and I won't tell a word."

He shuffled towards the door, but Athelney Jones got in front of him.

"Wait a bit, my friend," said he. "You have important information, and you must not walk off. We shall keep you, whether you like or not, until our friend returns."

The old man made a little run towards the door, but, as Athelney Jones put his broad back up against it, he recognized the uselessness of resistance.

"**Pretty** sort o' treatment this!" he cried, stamping his stick. "I come here to see a gentleman, and you two, who I never saw in my life, seize me and treat me in this fashion!"

"You will be **none the worse**," I said. "We shall **recompense** you for the loss of your time. Sit over here on the sofa, and you will not have long to wait."

He came across sullenly enough, and seated himself with his face resting on his hands. Jones and I resumed our cigars and our talk. Suddenly, however, Holmes's voice broke in upon us.

"I think that you might offer me a cigar too," he said.

We both started in our chairs. There was Holmes sitting close to us with an air of quiet amusement.

"Holmes!" I exclaimed. "You here! But where

disguise [disgáiz] n.
변장, 위장

workhouse [wɔ́:rkhàus] n.
빈민 수용시설, 강제 노역소
glint [glint] n.
반짝임, 번득임, 기미

getup [gétʌp] n.
복장, 옷차림

"Here is the old man," said he, holding out a heap of white hair.

is the old man?"

"Here is the old man," said he, holding out a heap of white hair. "Here he is—wig, whiskers, eyebrows, and all. I thought my **disguise** was pretty good, but I hardly expected that it would stand that test."

"Ah, You rogue!" cried Jones, highly delighted. "You would have made an actor, and a rare one. You had the proper **workhouse** cough, and those weak legs of yours are worth ten pound a week. I thought I knew the **glint** of your eye, though. You didn't get away from us so easily, You see."

"I have been working in that **get-up** all day," said he, lighting his cigar. "You see, a good many of the criminal classes begin to know me,—especially since our friend here took to publishing

some of my cases: so I can only go on the **war-path** under some simple disguise like this. You got my wire?"

"Yes; that was what brought me here."

"How has your case prospered?"

"It has all come to nothing. I have had to release two of my prisoners, and there is no evidence against the other two."

"Never mind. We shall give you two others in the place of them. But you must put yourself under my orders. You are welcome to all the official credit, but you must act on the lines that I point out. Is that agreed?"

"Entirely, if you will help me to the men."

"Well, then, in the first place I shall want a fast police-boat—a steam launch—to be at the Westminster Stairs at seven o'clock."

"That is easily managed. There is always one about there; but I can step across the road and telephone to make sure."

"Then I shall want two **stanch** men, in case of resistance."

"There will be two or three in the boat. What else?"

"When we secure the men we shall get the treasure. I think that it would be a pleasure to my friend here to take the box round to the young lady to whom half of it rightfully belongs. Let her be the first to open it. Eh, Watson?"

"It would be a great pleasure to me."

"Rather an irregular proceeding," said Jones, shaking his head.

"However, the whole thing is irregular, and I

wink at:
묵과하다, 못 본 체 하다

suppose we must **wink at** it. The treasure must afterwards be handed over to the authorities until after the official investigation."

"Certainly. That is easily managed. One other point. I should much like to have a few details about this matter from the lips of Jonathan Small himself. You know I like to work the detail of my cases out. There is no objection to my having an unofficial interview with him, either here in my rooms or elsewhere, as long as he is efficiently guarded?"

"Well, you are master of the situation. I have had no proof yet of the existence of this Jonathan Small. However, if you can catch him, I don't see how I can refuse you an interview with him."

"That is understood, then?"

"Perfectly. Is there anything else?"

"Only that I insist upon your dining with us. It will be ready in half an hour. I have oysters and a brace of grouse, with something a little choice in white wines. Watson, you have never yet recognized my merits as a housekeeper."

# 10 The End of the Islander

miracle play:
기적극, 중세의 종교적인 연극
medieval [mìːdíːv-əl, mèd-] adj.
중세의, 중세풍의
bon vivant [ɓɔːviːṽɑː] n.
(French) 미식가, 식도락가
elated [iléitid] adj.
우쭐한, 의기양양한

Our meal was a merry one. Holmes could talk exceedingly well when he chose, and that night he did choose. He appeared to be in a state of nervous exaltation. I have never known him so brilliant. He spoke on a quick succession of subjects,—on **miracle-plays**, on **medieval** pottery, on Stradivarius violins, on the Buddhism of Ceylon, and on the war-ships of the future,—handling each as though he had made a special study of it. His bright humor marked the reaction from his black depression of the preceding days. Athelney Jones proved to be a sociable soul in his hours of relaxation, and faced his dinner with the air of a ***bon vivant***. For myself, I felt **elated** at the thought that we were nearing the end of our task, and I

## 10 The End of the Islander

caught something of Holmes's **gaiety**. None of us alluded during dinner to the cause which had brought us together.

When the cloth was cleared, Holmes glanced at his watch, and filled up three glasses with **port**.

"One **bumper**," said he, "to the success of our little **expedition**. And now it is high time we were off. Have you a pistol, Watson?"

"I have my old service-revolver in my desk."

"You had best take it, then. It is well to be prepared. I see that the cab is at the door. I ordered it for half-past six."

It was a little past seven before we reached the Westminster **wharf**, and found our launch awaiting us. Holmes eyed it critically.

"Is there anything to mark it as a police-boat?"

"Yes; that green lamp at the side."

"Then **take** it **off**."

The small change was made, we stepped on board, and the ropes were cast off. Jones, Holmes, and I sat in the **stern**. There was one man at the **rudder**, one to tend the engines, and two **burly** police-inspectors forward.

"Where to?" asked Jones.

"To **the Tower**. Tell them to stop opposite Jacobson's Yard."

Our craft was evidently a very fast one. We shot past the long lines of loaded barges as though they were stationary. Holmes smiled with satisfaction as we **overhauled** a river steamer and left her behind us.

"We ought to be able to catch anything on the river," he said.

---

gaiety [géiəti] n.
명랑, 유쾌, 쾌활

port [pɔ:rt] n.
포트 와인
bumper [bʌ́mpəər] n.
건배, 가득찬 잔
expedition [èkspədíʃən] n.
(집단, 단체의) 모험, 원정

wharf [hwɔ:rf] n.
부두, 선창

take off:
떼어내다
stern [stə:rn] n.
고물, 선미 船尾
rudder [rʌ́də:r] n.
(배의) 키, 방향타
burly [bə́:rli] adj.
건장한, 우람한

the Tower:
런던탑

overhaul [òuvərhɔ́:l] v.
따라잡다, 앞지르다

clipper [klípər] n.
쾌속 범선
how the land lies:
형세, 상황
cf) see how the land lies 형세를 살피다
balk [bɔːk] v.
좌절시키다, 방해하다
scuttle [skátl] v.
고의로 배에 구멍을 내 침몰시키다
hypothesis [haipáθəsis / -pɔ́θ-] n.
가설 假說
cunning [kániŋ] n.
교활함, 간사함
finesse [finés] n.
예리함, 세밀함

"Well, hardly that. But there are not many launches to beat us."

"We shall have to catch the *Aurora*, and she has a name for being a **clipper**. I will tell you **how the land lies**, Watson. You recollect how annoyed I was at being **balked** by so small a thing?"

"Yes."

"Well, I gave my mind a thorough rest by plunging into a chemical analysis. One of our greatest statesmen has said that a change of work is the best rest. So it is. When I had succeeded in dissolving the hydrocarbon which I was at work at, I came back to the problem of the Sholtos, and thought the whole matter out again. My boys had been up the river and down the river without result. The launch was not at any landing-stage or wharf, nor had it returned. Yet it could hardly have been **scuttled** to hide their traces,—though that always remained as a possible **hypothesis** if all else failed. I knew that this man Small had a certain degree of low **cunning**, but I did not think him capable of anything in the nature of delicate **finesse**. That is usually a product of higher education. I then reflected that since he had certainly been in London some time—as we had evidence that he maintained a continual watch over Pondicherry Lodge—he could hardly leave at a moment's notice, but would need some little time, if it were only a day, to arrange his affairs. That was the balance of probability, at any rate."

"It seems to me to be a little weak," said I. "It is more probable that he had arranged his affairs before ever he set out upon his expedition."

## 10 The End of the Islander

lair [lɛə:r] n.
소굴, 은신처
strike [straik] v.
떠오르다, 생각나다

"No, I hardly think so. This **lair** of his would be too valuable a retreat in case of need for him to give it up until he was sure that he could do without it. But a second consideration **struck** me. Jonathan Small must have felt that the peculiar appearance of his companion, however much he may have top-coated him, would give rise to gossip, and possibly be associated with this Norwood tragedy. He was quite sharp enough to see that. They had started from their head-quarters under cover of darkness, and he would wish to get back before it was broad light. Now, it was past three o'clock, according to Mrs. Smith, when they got the boat. It would be quite bright, and people would be about in an hour or so. Therefore, I argued, they did not go very far. They paid Smith well to hold his tongue, reserved his launch for the final escape, and hurried to their lodgings with the treasure-box. In a couple of nights, when they had time to see what view the papers took, and whether there was any suspicion, they would make their way under cover of darkness to some ship at Gravesend or in the Downs, where no doubt they had already arranged for passages to America or the Colonies."

"But the launch? They could not have taken that to their lodgings."

"Quite so. I argued that the launch must be no great way off, in spite of its invisibility. I then put myself in the place of Small, and looked at it as a man of his capacity would. He would probably consider that to send back the launch or to keep it at a wharf would make pursuit easy if the police

in someone's shoes:
남의 입장에 서서

liable [láiəb-əl] adj.
~하기 쉬운
overlook [òuvərlúk] v.
모르고 지나치다
rig [rig] n.
복장, 옷차림
draw a blank:
실패로 끝나다, 허탕을 치다
rudder [rʌ́də:r] n.
(배의) 키, 방향타
naught [nɔːt, nɑːt ] n.
없음, 제로, 영
amiss [əmís] adj.
잘못된, 정상이 아닌
foreman [fɔ́ːrmən] n.
감독, 작업장, 십장
bellow [bélou] v.
소리지르다, 고함치다
flush [flʌʃ] adj.
풍족한, 풍부한

did happen to get on his track. How, then, could he conceal the launch and yet have her at hand when wanted? I wondered what I should do myself if I were **in his shoes**. I could only think of one way of doing it. I might hand the launch over to some boat-builder or repairer, with directions to make a trifling change in her. She would then be removed to his shed or yard, and so be effectually concealed, while at the same time I could have her at a few hours' notice."

"That seems simple enough."

"It is just these very simple things which are extremely **liable** to be **overlooked**. However, I determined to act on the idea. I started at once in this harmless seaman's **rig** and inquired at all the yards down the river. I **drew blank** at fifteen, but at the sixteenth—Jacobson's—I learned that the *Aurora* had been handed over to them two days ago by a wooden-legged man, with some trivial directions as to her **rudder**. 'There ain't **naught amiss** with her rudder,' said the **foreman**. 'There she lies, with the red streaks.' At that moment who should come down but Mordecai Smith, the missing owner? He was rather the worse for liquor. I should not, of course, have known him, but he **bellowed** out his name and the name of his launch. 'I want her to-night at eight o'clock,' said he,—'eight o'clock sharp, mind, for I have two gentlemen who won't be kept waiting.' They had evidently paid him well, for he was very **flush** of money, chucking shillings about to the men. I followed him some distance, but he subsided into an ale-house: so I went back to the yard, and, happening to pick up

# 10 The End of the Islander

one of my boys on the way, I stationed him as a **sentry** over the launch. He is to stand at water's edge and wave his handkerchief to us when they start. We shall be lying off in the stream, and it will be a strange thing if we do not take men, treasure, and all."

"You have planned it all very neatly, whether they are the right men or not," said Jones; "but if the affair were in my hands I should have had a body of police in Jacobson's Yard, and arrested them when they came down."

"Which would have been never. This man Small is a pretty **shrewd** fellow. He would send a scout on ahead, and if anything made him suspicious he would lie snug for another week."

"But you might have stuck to Mordecai Smith, and so been led to their hiding-place," said I.

"In that case I should have wasted my day. I think that it is a hundred to one against Smith knowing where they live. As long as he has liquor and good pay, why should he ask questions? They send him messages what to do. No, I thought over every possible course, and this is the best."

While this conversation had been proceeding, we had been shooting the long series of bridges which span the Thames. As we passed the City the last rays of the sun were **gilding** the cross upon the summit of St. Paul's. It was twilight before we reached the Tower.

"That is Jacobson's Yard," said Holmes, pointing to a bristle of masts and rigging on the Surrey side. "Cruise gently up and down here under cover of this string of lighters." He took a pair of night-glasses

---

sentry [séntri] n.
감시자, 파수, 보초

shrewd [ʃruːd] adj.
날카로운, 영리한

I wondered what I should do myself if I were in his shoes. I could only think of one way of doing it. I might hand the launch over to some boat-builder or repairer, with directions to make a trifling change in her.

gild [gild] v.
금박을 입히다, 치장하다

from his pocket and gazed some time at the shore. "I see my sentry at his post," he remarked, "but no sign of a handkerchief."

"Suppose we go down-stream a short way and lie in wait for them," said Jones, eagerly.

We were all eager by this time, even the policemen and **stokers**, who had a very vague idea of what was going forward.

"We have no right to **take anything for granted**," Holmes answered. "It is certainly ten to one that they go down-stream, but we cannot be certain. From this point we can see the entrance of the yard, and they can hardly see us. It will be a clear night and plenty of light. We must stay where we are. See how the folk swarm over **yonder** in the gaslight."

"They are coming from work in the yard."

"Dirty-looking rascals, but I suppose every one has some little immortal spark concealed about him. You would not think it, to look at them. There is no *a priori* probability about it. A strange **enigma** is man!"

"Some one calls him a soul concealed in an animal," I suggested.

"Winwood Reade is good upon the subject," said Holmes. "He remarks that, while the individual man is an **insoluble** puzzle, in the **aggregate** he becomes a mathematical certainty. You can, for example, never **foretell** what any one man will do, but you can say with precision what an average number will be up to. Individuals vary, but percentages remain constant. So says the **statistician**. But do I see a handkerchief? Surely there

## 10 The End of the Islander

flutter [flʌtəːr] n.
펄럭임

have/get the heels of:
추월하다, 앞서다

stoker [stóukəːr] n.
화부 火夫

whiz [hwiz] v.
칙칙 소리내다,
clank [klæŋk] v.
철컹거리다
prow [prau] n.
뱃머리, 이물
blur [bləːr] n.
희미한 형체
swirl [swəːrl] n.
소용돌이

is a white **flutter** over yonder."

"Yes, it is your boy," I cried. "I can see him plainly."

"And there is the *Aurora*," exclaimed Holmes, "and going like the devil! Full speed ahead, engineer. Make after that launch with the yellow light. By heaven, I shall never forgive myself if she proves to **have the heels of** us!"

She had slipped unseen through the yard-entrance and passed behind two or three small craft, so that she had fairly got her speed up before we saw her. Now she was flying down the stream, near in to the shore, going at a tremendous rate. Jones looked gravely at her and shook his head.

"She is very fast," he said. "I doubt if we shall catch her."

"We *must* catch her!" cried Holmes, between his teeth. "Heap it on, **stokers**! Make her do all she can! If we burn the boat we must have them!"

We were fairly after her now. The furnaces roared, and the powerful engines **whizzed** and **clanked**, like a great metallic heart. Her sharp, steep **prow** cut through the still river-water and sent two rolling waves to right and to left of us. With every throb of the engines we sprang and quivered like a living thing. One great yellow lantern in our bows threw a long, flickering funnel of light in front of us. Right ahead a dark **blur** upon the water showed where the *Aurora* lay, and the **swirl** of white foam behind her spoke of the pace at which she was going. We flashed past barges, steamers, merchant-vessels, in and out, behind this one and round the other. Voices hailed us out of

aquiline [ǽkwəlàin] adj.
독수리의, 매부리코의

tug [tʌg] n.
예인선
helm [helm] n.
타륜, 조타 장치

"We *must* catch her!" cried Holmes, between his teeth. "Heap it on, stokers! Make her do all she can! If we burn the boat we must have them!"

the darkness, but still the *Aurora* thundered on, and still we followed close upon her track.

"Pile it on, men, pile it on!" cried Holmes, looking down into the engine-room, while the fierce glow from below beat upon his eager, **aquiline** face. "Get every pound of steam you can."

"I think we gain a little," said Jones, with his eyes on the *Aurora*.

"I am sure of it," said I. "We shall be up with her in a very few minutes."

At that moment, however, as our evil fate would have it, a **tug** with three barges in tow blundered in between us. It was only by putting our **helm** hard down that we avoided a collision, and before we could round them and recover our way the *Aurora* had gained a good two hundred yards. She

# 10 The End of the Islander

murky [mə́:rki] adj.
어둑어둑한
starlit [stá:rlìt] adj.
별빛의, 별이 총총한
frail [freil] adj.
허약한
blur [blə:r] n.
희미한 형체
tiller [tílə:r] n.
키의 손잡이
checkered [tʃékərd] adj.
파란만장한
crouch [krautʃ] v.
구부리다, 쭈그리다, 움츠리다

It was only by putting our helm hard down that we avoided a collision, and before we could round them and recover our way the Aurora had gained a good two hundred yards.

was still, however, well in view, and the **murky** uncertain twilight was settling into a clear **starlit** night. Our boilers were strained to their utmost, and the **frail** shell vibrated and creaked with the fierce energy which was driving us along. We had shot through the Pool, past the West India Docks, down the long Deptford Reach, and up again after rounding the Isle of Dogs. The dull **blur** in front of us resolved itself now clearly enough into the dainty *Aurora*. Jones turned our search-light upon her, so that we could plainly see the figures upon her deck. One man sat by the stern, with something black between his knees over which he stooped. Beside him lay a dark mass which looked like a Newfoundland dog. The boy held the **tiller**, while against the red glare of the furnace I could see old Smith, stripped to the waist, and shovelling coals for dear life. They may have had some doubt at first as to whether we were really pursuing them, but now as we followed every winding and turning which they took there could no longer be any question about it. At Greenwich we were about three hundred paces behind them. At Blackwall we could not have been more than two hundred and fifty. I have coursed many creatures in many countries during my **checkered** career, but never did sport give me such a wild thrill as this mad, flying man-hunt down the Thames. Steadily we drew in upon them, yard by yard. In the silence of the night we could hear the panting and clanking of their machinery. The man in the stern still **crouched** upon the deck, and his arms were moving as though he were busy, while every

tremendous [triméndəs] adj.
굉장한, 대단한, 무서운
hail [heil] n.
외침, 고함
stern [stəːrn] n.
고물, 선미 船尾
poise [pɔiz] v.
균형을 유지하다
astride [əstráid] adj, adv
두 다리를 벌린
strident [stráid-ənt] adj.
귀에 거슬리는, 삐걱거리는
shock [ʃɑk / ʃɔk] n.
(무성한) 머리털
disheveled, dishevelled
[diʃévəld] adj.
흐트러진, 헝클어진
bestiality [bèstʃiǽləti, bìːs- / bèsti-] n.
잔인성, 짐승같은 성질

quarry [kwɔ́ːri / kwɑ́ri] n.
사냥감, 공격의 대상

now and then he would look up and measure with a glance the distance which still separated us. Nearer we came and nearer. Jones yelled to them to stop. We were not more than four boat's lengths behind them, both boats flying at a **tremendous** pace. It was a clear reach of the river, with Barking Level upon one side and the melancholy Plumstead Marshes upon the other. At our **hail** the man in the **stern** sprang up from the deck and shook his two clinched fists at us, cursing the while in a high, cracked voice. He was a good-sized, powerful man, and as he stood **poising** himself with legs **astride,** I could see that, from the thigh downwards, there was but a wooden stump upon the right side. At the sound of his **strident,** angry cries, there was a movement in the huddled bundle upon the deck. It straightened itself into a little black man—the smallest I have ever seen—with a great, misshapen head and a **shock** of tangled, **dishevelled** hair. Holmes had already drawn his revolver, and I whipped out mine at the sight of this savage, distorted creature. He was wrapped in some sort of dark ulster or blanket, which left only his face exposed; but that face was enough to give a man a sleepless night. Never have I seen features so deeply marked with all **bestiality** and cruelty. His small eyes glowed and burned with a sombre light, and his thick lips were writhed back from his teeth, which grinned and chattered at us with a half animal fury.

"Fire if he raises his hand," said Holmes, quietly.

We were within a boat's-length by this time, and almost within touch of our **quarry.** I can see

# 10 The End of the Islander

unhallowed [ʌnhǽloud] adj.
사악한, 죄가 많은
dwarf [dwɔːrf] n.
소인 小人
gnash [næʃ] v.
(이를) 갈다

pluck [plʌk] v.
끄집어내다
venomous [vénəməs] adj.
악의 가득한, 독성의
menacing [ménəsiŋ] adj.
위협적인
glimmer [glímər] v.
희미하게 비치다
stagnant [stǽgnənt] adj.
(물 등이) 괴어서 썩은
fugitive [fjúːdʒətiv] n.
도주자, 도피자
sodden [sádn / sɔ́dn] adj.
흠뻑 젖은
impotent [ímpətənt] adj.
무력한, 전혀 무리한

the two of them now as they stood: the white man with his legs far apart, shrieking out curses, and the **unhallowed dwarf** with his hideous face, and his strong yellow teeth **gnashing** at us in the light of our lantern.

It was well that we had so clear a view of him. Even as we looked he **plucked** out from under his covering a short, round piece of wood, like a school-ruler, and clapped it to his lips. Our pistols rang out together. He whirled round, threw up his arms, and, with a kind of choking cough, fell sideways into the stream. I caught one glimpse of his **venomous**, **menacing** eyes amid the white swirl of the waters. At the same moment the wooden-legged man threw himself upon the rudder and put it hard down, so that his boat made straight in for the southern bank, while we shot past her stern, only clearing her by a few feet. We were round after her in an instant, but she was already nearly at the bank. It was a wild and desolate place, where the moon **glimmered** upon a wide expanse of marsh-land, with pools of **stagnant** water and beds of decaying vegetation. The launch, with a dull thud, ran up upon the mud-bank, with her bow in the air and her stern flush with the water. The **fugitive** sprang out, but his stump instantly sank its whole length into the **sodden** soil. In vain he struggled and writhed. Not one step could he possibly take either forwards or backwards. He yelled in **impotent** rage, and kicked frantically into the mud with his other foot, but his struggles only bored his wooden pin the deeper into the sticky bank. When we brought our launch

chest [tʃest] n.
보관용 상자
ill-omened [-óumənd] adj.
불길한, 불운한

alongside he was so firmly anchored that it was only by throwing the end of a rope over his shoulders that we were able to haul him out, and to drag him, like some evil fish, over our side. The two Smiths, father and son, sat sullenly in their launch, but came aboard meekly enough when commanded. The *Aurora* herself we hauled off and made fast to our stern. A solid iron **chest** of Indian workmanship stood upon the deck. This, there could be no question, was the same that had contained the **ill-omened** treasure of the Sholtos. There was no key, but it was of considerable weight, so we transferred it carefully to our own little cabin. As we steamed slowly up-stream again, we flashed our search-light in every direction, but there was no sign of the Islander. Somewhere in

Even as we looked he plucked out from under his covering a short, round piece of wood, like a school-ruler, and clapped it to his lips. Our pistols rang out together.

ooze [u:z] n.
진흙 바닥

hatchway [hǽtʃwèi] n.
출입구, 승강구

the dark **ooze** at the bottom of the Thames lie the bones of that strange visitor to our shores.

"See here," said Holmes, pointing to the wooden **hatchway**. "We were hardly quick enough with our pistols." There, sure enough, just behind where we had been standing, stuck one of those murderous darts which we knew so well. It must have whizzed between us at the instant we fired. Holmes smiled at it and shrugged his shoulders in his easy fashion, but I confess that it turned me sick to think of the horrible death which had passed so close to us that night.

There, sure enough, just behind where we had been standing, stuck one of those murderous darts which we knew so well.

# 11 The Great Agra Treasure

captive [kǽptiv] n.
포로, 죄수
repose [ripóuz] n.
휴식, 고요함, 침착
expression [ikspréʃən] n.
얼굴, 표정

O ur **captive** sat in the cabin opposite to the iron box which he had done so much and waited so long to gain. He was a sunburned, reckless-eyed fellow, with a net-work of lines and wrinkles all over his mahogany features, which told of a hard, open-air life. There was a singular prominence about his bearded chin which marked a man who was not to be easily turned from his purpose. His age may have been fifty or thereabouts, for his black, curly hair was thickly shot with gray. His face in **repose** was not an unpleasing one, though his heavy brows and aggressive chin gave him, as I had lately seen, a terrible **expression** when moved to anger. He sat now with his handcuffed hands upon his lap, and his head sunk

keen [ki:n] adj.
날카로운, 강렬한
twinkling [twíkliŋ] adj.
반짝이는, 빛나는
contained [kəntéind] adj.
침착한
countenance [káuntənəns] n.
얼굴 표정, 안색
gleam [gli:m] n.
빛남, 번쩍임
swing [swiŋ] v.
교수형 당하다
hellhound [ˊ-hàund] n.
사악한 인간, 지옥을 지키는 개,
케르베로스
welt [welt] v.
세게 때리다

upon his breast, while he looked with his **keen**, **twinkling** eyes at the box which had been the cause of his ill-doings. It seemed to me that there was more sorrow than anger in his rigid and **contained countenance**. Once he looked up at me with a **gleam** of something like humor in his eyes.

"Well, Jonathan Small," said Holmes, lighting a cigar, "I am sorry that it has come to this."

"And so am I, sir," he answered, frankly. "I don't believe that I can **swing** over the job. I give you my word on the book that I never raised hand against Mr. Sholto. It was that little **hell-hound** Tonga who shot one of his cursed darts into him. I had no part in it, sir. I was as grieved as if it had been my blood-relation. I **welted** the little devil with the slack end of the rope for it, but it

was done, and I could not **undo** it again."

"Have a cigar," said Holmes; "and you had best take a pull out of my flask, for you are very wet. How could you expect so small and weak a man as this black fellow to overpower Mr. Sholto and hold him while you were climbing the rope?"

"You seem to know as much about it as if you were there, sir. The truth is that I hoped to find the room clear. I knew the habits of the house pretty well, and it was the time when Mr. Sholto usually went down to his supper. I shall make no secret of the business. The best defence that I can make is just the simple truth. Now, if it had been the **old major** I would have swung for him with a light heart. I would have thought no more of knifing him than of smoking this cigar. But it's cursed hard that I should be **lagged** over this **young Sholto**, with whom I had no quarrel whatever."

"You are under the charge of Mr. Athelney Jones, of Scotland Yard. He is going to bring you up to my rooms, and I shall ask you for a true **account** of the matter. You must **make a clean breast** of it, for if you do I hope that I may be of use to you. I think I can prove that the poison acts so quickly that the man was dead before ever you reached the room."

"That he was, sir. I never got such a **turn** in my life as when I saw him grinning at me with his head on his shoulder as I climbed through the window. It fairly shook me, sir. I'd have half killed Tonga for it if he had not scrambled off. That was how he came to leave his club, and some of his darts, too, as he tells me, which I dare say helped to put you on our track; though how you kept on it is more than I can tell. I don't feel no **malice** against you for it. But it does seem a queer thing," he added, with a bitter smile, "that I, who have a fair claim to half a million of money, should spend the first half of my life building a **breakwater** in the Andamans, and am like to spend the other half digging drains at Dartmoor. It was an evil day for me when first I **clapped eyes upon** the merchant Achmet and had to do with the Agra treasure, which never brought anything but a curse yet upon the man who owned it. To him, it brought murder, to Major Sholto it brought fear and guilt, to me it has meant slavery for life."

At this moment Athelney Jones thrust his face and shoulders into the tiny cabin.

"Quite a family party," he remarked. "I think I shall have a pull at that flask, Holmes. Well, I think we may all congratulate each other. Pity we didn't take the other alive; but there was no choice. I say, Holmes, you must confess that you cut it rather fine. It was all we could do to overhaul her."

"All is well that ends well," said Holmes. "But I certainly did not know that the *Aurora* was such a **clipper**."

"Smith says she is one of the fastest launches on the river, and that if he had had another man to help him with the engines we should never have caught her. He swears he knew nothing of this Norwood business."

"Neither he did," cried our prisoner,—"not a word. I chose his launch because I heard that she was a flier. We told him nothing, but we paid him

---

malice [mǽlis] n.
악의, 적의
breakwater [bréikwɔ̀:tər, -wɑ̀t-] n.
방파제
clap eye on~:
우연히 눈에 띄다

clipper [klípər] n.
쾌속 범선

bound [baund] adj.
~행인, ~에 가기로 된

consequential [kànsikwénʃəl / kɔ̀n] adj.
젠체하는, 거드름 부리는

well, and he was to get something handsome if we reached our vessel, the *Esmeralda*, at Gravesend, outward **bound** for the Brazils."

"Well, if he has done no wrong we shall see that no wrong comes to him. If we are pretty quick in catching our men, we are not so quick in condemning them." It was amusing to notice how the **consequential** Jones was already beginning to give himself airs on the strength of the capture. From the slight smile which played over Sherlock Holmes's face, I could see that the speech had not been lost upon him.

"We will be at Vauxhall Bridge presently," said Jones, "and shall land you, Dr. Watson, with the treasure-box. I need hardly tell you that I am taking a very grave responsibility upon myself in doing this. It is most irregular; but of course an agreement is an agreement. I must, however, as a matter of duty, send an inspector with you, since you have so valuable a charge. You will drive, no doubt?"

"Yes, I shall drive."

inventory [ínvəntɔ̀:ri / -təri] n.
품목 일람, 상품 목록, 재산 목록

"It is a pity there is no key, that we may make an **inventory** first. You will have to break it open. Where is the key, my man?"

"At the bottom of the river," said Small, shortly.

"Hum! There was no use your giving this unnecessary trouble. We have had work enough already through you. However, doctor, I need not warn you to be careful. Bring the box back with you to the Baker Street rooms. You will find us there, on our way to the station."

They landed me at Vauxhall, with my heavy

## 11 The Great Agra Treasure

iron box, and with a **bluff**, genial inspector as my companion. A quarter of an hour's drive brought us to Mrs. Cecil Forrester's. The servant seemed surprised at so late a visitor. Mrs. Cecil Forrester was out for the evening, she explained, and likely to be very late. Miss Morstan, however, was in the drawing-room: so to the drawing-room I went, box in hand, leaving the obliging inspector in the cab.

She was seated by the open window, dressed in some sort of white **diaphanous** material, with a little touch of scarlet at the neck and waist. The soft light of a shaded lamp fell upon her as she leaned back in the basket chair, playing over her sweet, grave face, and tinting with a dull, metallic sparkle the rich coils of her luxuriant hair. One white arm and hand drooped over the side of the chair, and her whole pose and figure spoke of an absorbing **melancholy**. At the sound of my foot-fall she sprang to her feet, however, and a bright flush of surprise and of pleasure colored her pale cheeks.

"I heard a cab drive up," she said. "I thought that Mrs. Forrester had come back very early, but I never dreamed that it might be you. What news have you brought me?"

"I have brought something better than news," said I, putting down the box upon the table and speaking **jovially** and **boisterously**, though my heart was heavy within me. "I have brought you something which is worth all the news in the world. I have brought you a fortune."

She glanced at the iron box.

"Is that the treasure, then?" she asked, coolly

---

bluff [blʌf] adj.
무뚝뚝한

diaphanous [daiǽfənəs] adj.
아주 얇은, 내비치는
melancholy [mélənkàli / -kɔ̀li] n.
우울, 구슬픔, 애수

jovially [dʒóuviəli] adv.
쾌활하게, 명랑하게
boisterously [bɔ́istərəsli] adv.
떠들썩하게, 시끄럽게

**annuity** [ənjúːəti] n.
연금

**ring** [riŋ] n.
(어떤 특성을 나타내는) 울림, 느낌, 기미

**tax** [tæks] v.
무거운 부담을 지우다, 무리를 강요하다

**pray** [prei] v.
please, "I pray you"의 생략형, 바라건대, 아무쪼록

**recital** [risáitl] n.
상세한 설명

enough.

"Yes, this is the great Agra treasure. Half of it is yours and half is Thaddeus Sholto's. You will have a couple of hundred thousand each. Think of that! An **annuity** of ten thousand pounds. There will be few richer young ladies in England. Is it not glorious?"

I think that I must have been rather overacting my delight, and that she detected a hollow **ring** in my congratulations, for I saw her eyebrows rise a little, and she glanced at me curiously.

"If I have it," said she, "I owe it to you."

"No, no," I answered, "not to me, but to my friend Sherlock Holmes. With all the will in the world, I could never have followed up a clue which has **taxed** even his analytical genius. As it was, we very nearly lost it at the last moment."

"**Pray** sit down and tell me all about it, Dr. Watson," said she.

I narrated briefly what had occurred since I had seen her last,—Holmes's new method of search, the discovery of the *Aurora*, the appearance of Athelney Jones, our expedition in the evening, and the wild chase down the Thames. She listened with parted lips and shining eyes to my **recital** of our adventures. When I spoke of the dart which had so narrowly missed us, she turned so white that I feared that she was about to faint.

"It is nothing," she said, as I hastened to pour her out some water.

"I am all right again. It was a shock to me to hear that I had placed my friends in such horrible peril."

"That is all over," I answered. "It was nothing.

# 11 The Great Agra Treasure

leave [li:v] n.
(공식적인) 허가, 허락

indifferent [indífərənt] adj.
무관심한, 개의치 않는

poker [póukər] n.
부지깽이
hasp [hæsp, hɑ:sp] n.
걸쇠
wrought [rɔ:t] v.
work의 과거, 과거분사형,
worked의 예전 사용 형태

shred [ʃred] n.
조각, 파편
crumb [krʌm] n.
조각, 부스러기

I will tell you no more gloomy details. Let us turn to something brighter. There is the treasure. What could be brighter than that? I got **leave** to bring it with me, thinking that it would interest you to be the first to see it."

"It would be of the greatest interest to me," she said. There was no eagerness in her voice, however. It had struck her, doubtless, that it might seem ungracious upon her part to be **indifferent** to a prize which had cost so much to win.

"What a pretty box!" she said, stooping over it. "This is Indian work, I suppose?"

"Yes; it is Benares metal-work."

"And so heavy!" she exclaimed, trying to raise it. "The box alone must be of some value. Where is the key?"

"Small threw it into the Thames," I answered. "I must borrow Mrs. Forrester's **poker**."

There was in the front a thick and broad **hasp**, **wrought** in the image of a sitting Buddha. Under this I thrust the end of the poker and twisted it outward as a lever. The hasp sprang open with a loud snap. With trembling fingers I flung back the lid. We both stood gazing in astonishment. The box was empty!

No wonder that it was heavy. The iron-work was two-thirds of an inch thick all round. It was massive, well made, and solid, like a chest constructed to carry things of great price, but not one **shred** or **crumb** of metal or jewelry lay within it. It was absolutely and completely empty.

"The treasure is lost," said Miss Morstan, calmly.

As I listened to the words and realized what

weigh down:
짐이 되다, 부담이 되다
save [seiv] prep.
except, ~을 제외하고

they meant, a great shadow seemed to pass from my soul. I did not know how this Agra treasure had **weighed** me **down**, until now that it was finally removed. It was selfish, no doubt, disloyal, wrong, but I could realize nothing **save** that the golden barrier was gone from between us.

"Thank God!" I ejaculated from my very heart.

She looked at me with a quick, questioning smile.

"Why do you say that?" she asked.

"Because you are within my reach again," I said, taking her hand. She did not withdraw it. "Because I love you, Mary, as truly as ever a man loved a woman. Because this treasure, these riches, sealed my lips. Now that they are gone I can tell you how I love you. That is why I said, 'Thank God.'"

"Then I say, 'Thank God,' too," she whispered,

It was selfish, no doubt, disloyal, wrong, but I could realize nothing save that the golden barrier was gone from between us.

as I drew her to my side.

Whoever had lost a treasure, I knew that night that I had gained one.

# 12 The Strange Story of Jonathan Small

A very patient man was that inspector in the cab, for it was a weary time before I rejoined him. His face clouded over when I showed him the empty box.

"There goes the reward!" said he, gloomily. "Where there is no money there is no pay. This night's work would have been worth a **tenner** each to Sam Brown and me if the treasure had been there."

"Mr. Thaddeus Sholto is a rich man," I said. "He will see that you are rewarded, treasure or no."

The inspector shook his head **despondently**, however.

"It's a bad job," he repeated; "and so Mr. Athelney Jones will think."

listless [lístlis] adj.
무관심한, 굼뜬
stolidly [stálidli / stɔ́l-] adv.
무감동하게, 둔감하게

loot [lu:t] n.
약탈품, 장물
kith and kin [kiθ--] n.
일가친척
rupee [ru:píː] n.
인도 등지의 화폐 단위

His forecast proved to be correct, for the detective looked blank enough when I got to Baker Street and showed him the empty box. They had only just arrived, Holmes, the prisoner, and he, for they had changed their plans so far as to report themselves at a station upon the way. My companion lounged in his arm-chair with his usual **listless** expression, while Small sat **stolidly** opposite to him with his wooden leg cocked over his sound one. As I exhibited the empty box he leaned back in his chair and laughed aloud.

"This is your doing, Small," said Athelney Jones, angrily.

"Yes, I have put it away where you shall never lay hand upon it," he cried, exultantly. "It is my treasure; and if I can't have the **loot** I'll take darned good care that no one else does. I tell you that no living man has any right to it, unless it is three men who are in the Andaman convict-barracks and myself. I know now that I cannot have the use of it, and I know that they cannot. I have acted all through for them as much as for myself. It's been the sign of four with us always. Well I know that they would have had me do just what I have done, and throw the treasure into the Thames rather than let it go to **kith or kin** of Sholto or of Morstan. It was not to make them rich that we did for Achmet. You'll find the treasure where the key is, and where little Tonga is. When I saw that your launch must catch us, I put the loot away in a safe place. There are no **rupees** for you this journey."

"You are deceiving us, Small," said Athelney Jones, sternly. "If you had wished to throw the

shrewd [ʃruːd] adj.
날카로운, 영리한
sidelong [-lɔ̀ːŋ / -lɔ̀ŋ] adj.
옆의, 옆으로 향한, 비스듬한
cry over spilled(spilt) milk:
지나간 일을 후회하다

thwart [θwɔːrt] v.
훼방놓다, 방해하다

snarl [snɑːrl] v.
성내며 말하다, 위협조로 말하다
pretty [príti] adj.
상당히 나쁜, 끔찍한, 형편없는
filthy [fílθi] adj.
더러운, 불결한
rack [ræk] v.
심한 고통을 주다, 괴롭히다
ague [éigjuː] n.
말라리아열, 학질
bully [búli] v.
못살게 굴다, 을러메다
take it out of someone:
화풀이 하다, 진력나게 하다
hide [haid] n.
피부, 목숨

treasure into the Thames, it would have been easier for you to have thrown box and all."

"Easier for me to throw, and easier for you to recover," he answered, with a **shrewd, sidelong** look. "The man that was clever enough to hunt me down is clever enough to pick an iron box from the bottom of a river. Now that they are scattered over five miles or so, it may be a harder job. It went to my heart to do it, though. I was half mad when you came up with us. However, there's no good grieving over it. I've had ups in my life, and I've had downs, but I've learned not to **cry over spilled milk**."

"This is a very serious matter, Small," said the detective. "If you had helped justice, instead of **thwarting** it in this way, you would have had a better chance at your trial."

"Justice!" **snarled** the ex-convict. "A **pretty** justice! Whose loot is this, if it is not ours? Where is the justice that I should give it up to those who have never earned it? Look how I have earned it! Twenty long years in that fever-ridden swamp, all day at work under the mangrove-tree, all night chained up in the **filthy** convict-huts, bitten by mosquitoes, **racked** with **ague**, **bullied** by every cursed black-faced policeman who loved to **take it out of a white man**. That was how I earned the Agra treasure; and you talk to me of justice because I cannot bear to feel that I have paid this price only that another may enjoy it! I would rather swing a score of times, or have one of Tonga's darts in my **hide**, than live in a convict's cell and feel that another man is at his ease in a palace

## 12 The Strange Story of Jonathan Small

with the money that should be mine."

Small had dropped his mask of **stoicism**, and all this came out in a wild whirl of words, while his eyes blazed, and the handcuffs **clanked** together with the impassioned movement of his hands. I could understand, as I saw the fury and the passion of the man, that it was no **groundless** or unnatural terror which had possessed Major Sholto when he first learned that the injured convict was upon his track.

"You forget that we know nothing of all this," said Holmes quietly.

"We have not heard your story, and we cannot tell how far justice may originally have been on your side."

"Well, sir, you have been very **fair-spoken** to me, though I can see that I have you to thank that I have these bracelets upon my wrists. Still, I **bear no grudge** for that. It is all fair and **above-board**. If you want to hear my story I have no wish to hold it back. What I say to you is God's truth, every word of it. Thank you; you can put the glass beside me here, and I'll put my lips to it if I am dry.

"I am a Worcestershire man myself, born near Pershore. I dare say you would find a heap of Smalls living there now if you were to look. I have often thought of taking a look round there, but the truth is that I was never much of a **credit** to the family, and I doubt if they would be so very glad to see me. They were all steady, chapel-going folk, small farmers, well known and respected over the country-side, while I was always a bit of a **rover**. At last, however, when I was about

---

stoicism [stóuəsìz-əm] n.
냉철함, 극기, 스토아 주의
clank [klæŋk] v.
철컹거리다
groundless [gráundlis] adj.
근거없는, 사실 무근의

fair-spoken [-spóukən] adj.
말씨가 정중한
bear a grudge:
원한을 품다
aboveboard [əbávbɔ̀:rd] adj.
분명한, 정직한

credit [krédit] n.
명예가 되는 것, 영예
rover [róuvə:r] n.
유랑자, 방랑자

Small had dropped his mask of stoicism, and all this came out in a wild whirl of words, ...

eighteen, I gave them no more trouble, for I got into a mess over a girl, and could only get out of it again by taking the queen's shilling and joining the 3rd Buffs, which was just starting for India.

"I wasn't destined to do much soldiering, however. I had just got past the **goose-step**, and learned to handle my **musket**, when I was fool enough to go swimming in the Ganges. Luckily for me, my company sergeant, John Holder, was in the water at the same time, and he was one of the finest swimmers in the service. A crocodile took me, just as I was half-way across, and nipped off my right leg as clean as a surgeon could have done it, just above the knee. What with the shock and the loss of blood, I fainted, and should have drowned if Holder had not caught hold of me and paddled for the bank. I was five months in hospital over it, and when at last I was able to limp out of it with this timber toe strapped to my stump I found myself **invalided** out of the army and unfitted for any active occupation.

"I was, as you can imagine, pretty down on my luck at this time, for I was a useless **cripple** though not yet in my twentieth year. However, my misfortune soon proved to be a **blessing in disguise**. A man named Abelwhite, who had come out there as an indigo-planter, wanted an **overseer** to look after his **coolies** and keep them up to their work. He happened to be a friend of our colonel's, who had taken an interest in me since the accident. To make a long story short, the colonel recommended me strongly for the post and, as the work was mostly to be done on horseback, my leg was no

## 12 The Strange Story of Jonathan Small

plantation [plæntéiʃən] n.
농장, 농원
quarters [kwɔ́:rtər] n.
숙소, 주거
shanty [ʃǽnti] n.
오두막집

mutiny [mjú:t-əni] n.
반란, 폭동
cf) 세포이 항쟁
obstinate [ábstənit / ɔ́b-] adj.
완고한, 외고집의

great obstacle, for I had enough knee left to keep a good grip on the saddle. What I had to do was to ride over the **plantation**, to keep an eye on the men as they worked, and to report the idlers. The pay was fair, I had comfortable **quarters**, and altogether I was content to spend the remainder of my life in indigo-planting. Mr. Abel White was a kind man, and he would often drop into my little **shanty** and smoke a pipe with me, for white folk out there feel their hearts warm to each other as they never do here at home.

"Well, I was never in luck's way long. Suddenly, without a note of warning, the great **mutiny** broke upon us. One month India lay as still and peaceful, to all appearance, as Surrey or Kent; the next there were two hundred thousand black devils let loose, and the country was a perfect hell. Of course you know all about it, gentlemen,—a deal more than I do, very like, since reading is not in my line. I only know what I saw with my own eyes. Our plantation was at a place called Muttra, near the border of the Northwest Provinces. Night after night the whole sky was alight with the burning bungalows, and day after day we had small companies of Europeans passing through our estate with their wives and children, on their way to Agra, where were the nearest troops. Mr. Abelwhite was an **obstinate** man. He had it in his head that the affair had been exaggerated, and that it would blow over as suddenly as it had sprung up. There he sat on his veranda, drinking whiskey-pegs and smoking cheroots, while the country was in a blaze about him. Of course we stuck by him, I and

nullah [nʌ́lə] n.
수로
rein [rein] v.
고삐로 제어하다, 고삐를 당기다

Dawson, who, with his wife, used to do the bookwork and the managing. Well, one fine day the crash came. I had been away on a distant plantation, and was riding slowly home in the evening, when my eye fell upon something all huddled together at the bottom of a steep **nullah**. I rode down to see what it was, and the cold struck through my heart when I found it was Dawson's wife, all cut into ribbons, and half eaten by jackals and native dogs. A little further up the road Dawson himself was lying on his face, quite dead, with an empty revolver in his hand and four Sepoys lying across each other in front of him. I **reined** up my horse, wondering which way I should turn; but at that moment I saw thick smoke curling up from Abel White's bungalow, and the flames

meddle [médl] v.
간섭하다
fiends [fi:nd] n.
악한, 악령
paddy [pǽdi] n.
쌀, 벼

fugitive [fjú:dʒətiv] n.
도주자, 도피자
bugle [bjú:gəl] n.
군대 나팔

beginning to burst through the roof. I knew then that I could do my employer no good, but would only throw my own life away if I **meddled** in the matter. From where I stood I could see hundreds of the black **fiends**, with their red coats still on their backs, dancing and howling round the burning house. Some of them pointed at me, and a couple of bullets sang past my head; so I broke away across the **paddy**-fields, and found myself late at night safe within the walls at Agra.

"As it proved, however, there was no great safety here, either. The whole country was up like a swarm of bees. Wherever the English could collect in little bands, they held just the ground that their guns commanded. Everywhere else they were helpless **fugitives**. It was a fight of the millions against the hundreds; and the cruellest part of it was that these men that we fought against, foot, horse, and gunners, were our own picked troops, whom we had taught and trained, handling our own weapons, and blowing our own **bugle**-calls. At Agra there were the 3rd Bengal Fusiliers, some Sikhs, two troops of horse, and a battery of artillery. A volunteer corps of clerks and merchants had been formed, and this I joined, wooden leg and all. We went out to meet the rebels at Shahgunge early in July, and we beat them back for a time, but our powder gave out, and we had to fall back upon the city.

"Nothing but the worst news came to us from every side—which is not to be wondered at, for if you look at the map you will see that we were right in the heart of it. Lucknow is rather better than a hundred miles to the east, and Cawnpore about as far to the south. From every point on the compass there was nothing but torture and murder and outrage.

"The city of Agra is a great place, swarming with fanatics and fierce devil-worshippers of all sorts. Our handful of men were lost among the narrow, winding streets. Our leader moved across the river, therefore, and took up his position in the old **fort** at Agra. I don't know if any of you gentlemen have ever read or heard anything of that old fort. It is a very queer place—the queerest that ever I was in, and I have been in some **rum** corners, too. First of all, it is enormous in size. I should think that the enclosure must be acres and acres. There is a modern part, which took all our garrison, women, children, stores, and everything else, with plenty of room over. But the modern part is nothing like the size of the old quarter, where nobody goes, and which is given over to the scorpions and the centipedes. It is all full of great deserted halls, and winding passages, and long corridors twisting in and out, so that it is easy enough for folk to get lost in it. For this reason it was seldom that any one went into it, though now and again a party with torches might go exploring.

"The river washes along the front of the old fort, and so protects it, but on the sides and behind there are many doors, and these had to be guarded, of course, in the old quarter as well as in that which was actually held by our troops. We were **short-handed**, with hardly men enough to **man** the **angles** of the building and to serve the guns.

## 12 The Strange Story of Jonathan Small

innumerable [injú:mərəbəl] adj.
무수한, 셀 수 없이 많은
take charge:
책임을 지다, 임무를 맡다
labyrinth [lǽbərìnθ] n.
미로 迷路

raw [rɔː] adj.
숙련되지 않은, 경험이 많지 않은
game [geim] adj.
절름발이의, 불구의
at that:
게다가
jabber [dʒǽbər] v.
불분명하게 지껄이다
lingo [líŋgou] n.
지방어, 사투리, 특정 언어
tomtom [támtàm / tɔ́mtɔ̀m] n.
작은 드럼

It was impossible for us, therefore, to station a strong guard at every one of the **innumerable** gates. What we did was to organize a central guard-house in the middle of the fort, and to leave each gate under the charge of one white man and two or three natives. I was selected to **take charge** during certain hours of the night of a small isolated door upon the southwest side of the building. Two Sikh troopers were placed under my command, and I was instructed if anything went wrong to fire my musket, when I might rely upon help coming at once from the central guard. As the guard was a good two hundred paces away, however, and as the space between was cut up into a **labyrinth** of passages and corridors, I had great doubts as to whether they could arrive in time to be of any use in case of an actual attack.

"Well, I was pretty proud at having this small command given me, since I was a **raw** recruit, and a **game**-legged one **at that**. For two nights I kept the watch with my Punjaubees. They were tall, fierce-looking chaps, Mahomet Singh and Abdullah Khan by name, both old fighting-men who had borne arms against us at Chilian-wallah. They could talk English pretty well, but I could get little out of them. They preferred to stand together and **jabber** all night in their queer Sikh **lingo**. For myself, I used to stand outside the gate-way, looking down on the broad, winding river and on the twinkling lights of the great city. The beating of drums, the rattle of **tomtoms**, and the yells and howls of the rebels, drunk with opium and with bhang, were enough to remind us all night of our dangerous neighbors across the stream.

Every two hours the officer of the night used to come round to all the posts, to make sure that all was well.

"The third night of my watch was dark and dirty, with a small, driving rain. It was dreary work standing in the gate-way hour after hour in such weather. I tried again and again to make my Sikhs talk, but without much success. At two in the morning the rounds passed, and broke for a moment the weariness of the night. Finding that my companions would not be led into conversation, I took out my pipe, and laid down my musket to strike the match. In an instant the two Sikhs were upon me. One of them snatched my **firelock** up and **levelled** it at my head, while the other held a great knife to my throat and swore between his teeth that he would plunge it into me if I moved a step.

"My first thought was that these fellows were **in league with** the **rebels**, and that this was the beginning of an assault. If our door were in the hands of the Sepoys the place must fall, and the women and children be treated as they were in Cawnpore. Maybe you gentlemen think that I am just making out a case for myself, but I give you my word that when I thought of that, though I felt the point of the knife at my throat, I opened my mouth with the intention of giving a scream, if it was my last one, which might alarm the main guard. The man who held me seemed to know my thoughts; for, even as I **braced** myself to it, he whispered, 'Don't make a noise. The fort is safe

firelock [-lə̀k / -lɔ̀k] n.
화승총
level [lév-əl] v.
겨누다, 겨냥하다, 돌리다

in league with~:
~와 동맹하여, 결탁하여, 공모하여
rebel [réb-əl] n.
반역자, 반란자, 모반자
brace [breis] v.
긴장하다, 대비하다, 마음을 다잡다

ring [riŋ] n.
(어떤 특성을 나타내는) 울림, 느낌, 기미

sahib [sáːhib] n.
(in India) sir; master 인도인이 쓰던 유럽인에 대한 존칭

There is no middle way. Which is it to be, death or life?

enough. There are no rebel dogs on this side of the river.' There was the **ring** of truth in what he said, and I knew that if I raised my voice I was a dead man. I could read it in the fellow's brown eyes. I waited, therefore, in silence, to see what it was that they wanted from me.

"'Listen to me, **Sahib**,' said the taller and fiercer of the pair, the one whom they called Abdullah Khan. 'You must either be with us now or you must be silenced forever. The thing is too great a one for us to hesitate. Either you are heart and soul with us on your oath on the cross of the Christians, or your body this night shall be thrown into the ditch and we shall pass over to our brothers in the rebel army. There is no middle way. Which is it to be, death or life? We can only give

fort [fɔ:rt] n.
성채, 보루
truck [trʌk] n.
거래

loot [lu:t] n.
약탈품, 장물

provided: conj.
만약 ~이면

you three minutes to decide, for the time is passing, and all must be done before the rounds come again.'

"'How can I decide?' said I. 'You have not told me what you want of me. But I tell you now that if it is anything against the safety of the **fort** I will have no **truck** with it, so you can drive home your knife and welcome.'

"'It is nothing against the fort,' said he. 'We only ask you to do that which your countrymen come to this land for. We ask you to be rich. If you will be one of us this night, we will swear to you upon the naked knife, and by the threefold oath which no Sikh was ever known to break, that you shall have your fair share of the **loot**. A quarter of the treasure shall be yours. We can say no fairer.'

"'But what is the treasure, then?' I asked. 'I am as ready to be rich as you can be, if you will but show me how it can be done.'

"'You will swear, then,' said he, 'by the bones of your father, by the honor of your mother, by the cross of your faith, to raise no hand and speak no word against us, either now or afterwards?'

"'I will swear it,' I answered, '**provided** that the fort is not endangered.'

"'Then my comrade and I will swear that you shall have a quarter of the treasure which shall be equally divided among the four of us.'

"'There are but three,' said I.

"'No; Dost Akbar must have his share. We can tell the tale to you while we await them. Do you stand at the gate, Mahomet Singh, and give notice of their coming. The thing stands thus, Sahib,

feringhee [fəríŋgi] n.
(Indian) 유럽사람
Had you been~:
If you had been~
hearken [háːrkən] v.
경청하다, 귀를 기울이다

raja, rajah [ráːdʒə] n.
인도의 군주, 국왕, 우두머리
hoard [hɔːrd] v.
모으다
Company [kʌ́mpəni]:
East India Company, 동인도회사
raj [rɑːdʒ] n.
(인도에서의) 지배, 통치

and I tell it to you because I know that an oath is binding upon a **Feringhee**, and that we may trust you. **Had you been** a lying Hindoo, though you had sworn by all the gods in their false temples, your blood would have been upon the knife and your body in the water. But the Sikh knows the Englishman, and the Englishman knows the Sikh. **Hearken**, then, to what I have to say.

"'There is a **rajah** in the northern provinces who has much wealth, though his lands are small. Much has come to him from his father, and more still he has set by himself, for he is of a low nature, and **hoards** his gold rather than spend it. When the troubles broke out he would be friends both with the lion and the tiger—with the Sepoy and with the **Company**'s **Raj**. Soon, however, it seemed to him that the white men's day was come, for through all the land he could hear of nothing but of their death and their overthrow. Yet, being a careful man, he made such plans that, come what might, half at least of his treasure should be left to him. That which was in gold and silver he kept by him in the vaults of his palace, but the most precious stones and the choicest pearls that he had he put in an iron box, and sent it by a trusty servant who, under the guise of a merchant, should take it to the fort at Agra, there to lie until the land is at peace. Thus, if the rebels won he would have his money, but if the Company conquered his jewels would be saved to him. Having thus divided his hoard, he threw himself into the cause of the Sepoys, since they were strong upon his borders. By doing this, mark you, Sahib, his

**true to one's salt:**
직무에 충실한

**postern** [póustə:rn, pás-] n.
뒷문, 샛문

**ne'er-do-well** [nέərdu:wèl], [-wìː l] n.
쓸모없는 사람, 건달

**moidore** [mɔ́idɔːr] n.
모이도르, 포르투갈 및 브라질의 옛 금화

**commandant** [kámənda̒ent, -dɑ́:nt / kɔ̀mənda̒ent, -dɑ́:nt] n.
사령관, 지휘관

property becomes the due of those who have been **true to their salt.**

"'This pretended merchant, who travels under the name of Achmet, is now in the city of Agra, and desires to gain his way into the fort. He has with him as travelling-companion my foster-brother Dost Akbar, who knows his secret. Dost Akbar has promised this night to lead him to a side-**postern** of the fort, and has chosen this one for his purpose. Here he will come presently, and here he will find Mahomet Singh and myself awaiting him. The place is lonely, and none shall know of his coming. The world shall know of the merchant Achmet no more, but the great treasure of the rajah shall be divided among us. What say you to it, Sahib?'

"In Worcestershire the life of a man seems a great and a sacred thing; but it is very different when there is fire and blood all round you, and you have been used to meeting death at every turn. Whether Achmet, the merchant, lived or died was a thing as light as air to me, but at the talk about the treasure my heart turned to it, and I thought of what I might do in the old country with it, and how my folk would stare when they saw their **ne'er-do-well** coming back with his pockets full of gold **moidores**. I had, therefore, already made up my mind. Abdullah Khan, however, thinking that I hesitated, pressed the matter more closely.

"'Consider, Sahib,' said he, 'that if this man is taken by the **commandant** he will be hung or shot, and his jewels taken by the government, so that no man will be a rupee the better for them. Now, since we do the taking of him, why should we not

## 12 The Strange Story of Jonathan Small

do the rest as well? The jewels will be as well with us as in the Company's **coffers**. There will be enough to make every one of us rich men and great chiefs. No one can know about the matter, for here we are cut off from all men. What could be better for the purpose? Say again, then, Sahib, whether you are with us, or if we must look upon you as an enemy.'

"'I am with you heart and soul,' said I.

"'It is well,' he answered, handing me back my firelock. 'You see that we trust you, for your word, like ours, is not to be broken. We have now only to wait for my brother and the merchant.'

"'Does your brother know, then, of what you will do?' I asked.

"'The plan is his. He has devised it. We will go to the gate and share the watch with Mahomet Singh.'

"The rain was still falling steadily, for it was just the beginning of the wet season. Brown, heavy clouds were drifting across the sky, and it was hard to see more than a stone-cast. A deep **moat** lay in front of our door, but the water was in places nearly dried up, and it could easily be crossed. It was strange to me to be standing there with those two wild Punjaubees waiting for the man who was coming to his death.

"Suddenly my eye caught the **glint** of a shaded lantern at the other side of the moat. It vanished among the mound-heaps, and then appeared again coming slowly in our direction.

"'Here they are!' I exclaimed.

"'You will **challenge** him, Sahib, as usual,' whispered Abdullah. 'Give him no cause for fear. Send

coffer [kɔ́:fər, káf-] n.
금고, 재원

moat [mout] n.
해자 垓字

glint [glint] n.
반짝임, 번득임, 기미

challenge [tʃǽlindʒ] v.
수하(誰何)하다, 검문하다

mire [maiər] n.
늪

friend [frend] n.
자기편, 아군, 전우, 동료

cummerbund [kʌ́mərbʌ̀nd] n.
허리띠

us in with him, and we shall do the rest while you stay here on guard. Have the lantern ready to uncover, that we may be sure that it is indeed the man.'

"The light had flickered onwards, now stopping and now advancing, until I could see two dark figures upon the other side of the moat. I let them scramble down the sloping bank, splash through the **mire**, and climb half-way up to the gate, before I challenged them.

"'Who goes there?' said I, in a subdued voice.

"'**Friends**,' came the answer. I uncovered my lantern and threw a flood of light upon them. The first was an enormous Sikh, with a black beard which swept nearly down to his **cummerbund**. Outside of a show I have never seen so tall a man. The other was a little, fat, round fellow, with a great yellow turban, and a bundle in his hand, done up in a shawl. He seemed to be all in a quiver with fear, for his hands twitched as if he had the ague, and his head kept turning to left and right with two bright little twinkling eyes, like a mouse when he ventures out from his hole. It gave me the chills to think of killing him, but I thought of the treasure, and my heart set as hard as a flint within me. When he saw my white face he gave a little chirrup of joy and came running up towards me.

"'Your protection, Sahib,' he panted; 'your protection for the unhappy merchant Achmet. I have travelled across Rajpootana that I might seek the shelter of the fort at Agra. I have been robbed and beaten and abused because I have been the friend of the Company. It is a blessed night this when I am once more in safety—I and my poor possessions.'

"'What have you in the bundle?' I asked.

"'An iron box,' he answered, 'which contains one or two little family matters which are of no value to others, but which I should be sorry to lose. Yet I am not a beggar; and I shall reward you, young Sahib, and your governor also, if he will give me the shelter I ask.'

"I could not trust myself to speak longer with the man. The more I looked at his fat, frightened face, the harder did it seem that we should slay him in cold blood. It was best to get it over.

"'Take him to the main guard,' said I. The two Sikhs closed in upon him on each side, and the giant walked behind, while they marched in through the dark gateway. Never was a man so compassed round with death. I remained at the gateway with the lantern.

"I could hear the measured tramp of their footsteps sounding through the lonely corridors. Suddenly it ceased, and I heard voices, and a scuffle, with the sound of blows. A moment later there came, to my horror, a rush of footsteps coming in my direction, with the loud breathing of a running man. I turned my lantern down the long, straight passage, and there was the fat man, running like the wind, with a smear of blood across his face, and close at his heels, bounding like a tiger, the great black-bearded Sikh, with a knife flashing in his hand. I have never seen a man run so fast as that little merchant. He was gaining on the Sikh, and I could see that if he once passed me and got to the open air he would save himself yet. My heart softened to him, but again the thought of his treasure turned me hard and bitter. I cast my firelock between his legs as he raced past, and he rolled twice over like a shot rabbit. Ere he could stagger to his feet the Sikh was upon him, and buried his knife twice in his side. The man never uttered moan nor moved muscle, but lay where he had fallen. I think myself that he may have broken his neck with the fall. You see, gentlemen, that I am keeping my promise. I am telling you every word of the business just exactly as it happened, whether it is in my favor or not."

He stopped, and held out his manacled hands for the whiskey-and-water which Holmes had brewed for him. For myself, I confess that I had

## 12 The Strange Story of Jonathan Small

flippant [flípənt] adj.
경박한, 성의 없는
in store:
다가오는, 박두하는, 준비된

now conceived the utmost horror of the man, not only for this cold-blooded business in which he had been concerned, but even more for the somewhat **flippant** and careless way in which he narrated it. Whatever punishment was **in store** for him, I felt that he might expect no sympathy from me. Sherlock Holmes and Jones sat with their hands upon their knees, deeply interested in the story, but with the same disgust written upon their faces. He may have observed it, for there was a touch of defiance in his voice and manner as he proceeded.

"It was all very bad, no doubt," said he. "I should like to know how many fellows in my shoes would have refused a share of this loot when they knew that they would have their throats cut for their pains. Besides, it was my life or his when once he was in the fort. If he had got out, the whole business would come to light, and I should have been **court-martialled** and shot as likely as not; for people were not very **lenient** at a time like that."

court-martial [-má:rʃəl] v.
군법 회의에 회부되다
lenient [líːniənt, -njənt] adj.
관대한

"Go on with your story," said Holmes, shortly.

"Well, we carried him in, Abdullah, Akbar, and I. A fine weight he was, too, for all that he was so short. Mahomet Singh was left to guard the door. We took him to a place which the Sikhs had already prepared. It was some distance off, where a winding passage leads to a great empty hall, the brick walls of which were all crumbling to pieces. The earth floor had sunk in at one place, making a natural grave, so we left Achmet the merchant there, having first covered him over with loose bricks. This done, we all went back to the treasure.

water [wɔ́ːtəːr, wɑ́t-] n.
품질, 우수성

"It lay where he had dropped it when he was first attacked. The box was the same which now lies open upon your table. A key was hung by a silken cord to that carved handle upon the top. We opened it, and the light of the lantern gleamed upon a collection of gems such as I have read of and thought about when I was a little lad at Pershore. It was blinding to look upon them. When we had feasted our eyes we took them all out and made a list of them. There were one hundred and forty-three diamonds of the first **water**, including one which has been called, I believe, 'the Great Mogul' and is said to be the second largest stone in existence. Then there were ninety-seven very fine emeralds, and one hundred and seventy rubies, some of which, however, were small. There were forty carbuncles, two hundred and ten sapphires, sixty-one agates, and a great quantity of beryls, onyxes, cats'-eyes, turquoises, and other stones, the very names of which I did not know at the time, though I have become more familiar with them since. Besides this, there were nearly three hundred very fine pearls, twelve of which were set in a gold coronet. By the way, these last had been taken out of the chest and were not there when I recovered it.

solemnly [sɑ́ləmli / sɔ́l-] adv.
진지하게, 엄숙하게
renew [rinjúː] v.
다시 하다, 되풀이하다
oath [ouθ] n.
서약, 맹세

"After we had counted our treasures we put them back into the chest and carried them to the gateway to show them to Mahomet Singh. Then we **solemnly renewed** our **oath** to stand by each other and be true to our secret. We agreed to conceal our loot in a safe place until the country should be at peace again, and then to divide it equally among ourselves. There was no use dividing it at present, for if gems of such value were found upon us it would cause suspicion, and there was no privacy in the fort nor any place where we could keep them. We carried the box, therefore, into the same hall where we had buried the body, and there, under certain bricks in the best-preserved wall, we made a hollow and put our treasure. We made careful note of the place, and next day I drew four plans, one for each of us, and put the sign of the four of us at the bottom, for we had sworn that we should each always act for all, so that none might take advantage. That is an oath that I can put my hand to my heart and swear that I have never broken.

"Well, there's no use my telling you gentlemen what came of the Indian mutiny. After Wilson took Delhi and Sir Colin relieved Lucknow the back of the business was broken. Fresh troops came pouring in, and Nana Sahib made himself scarce over the frontier. A flying column under Colonel Greathed came round to Agra and cleared the Pandies away from it. Peace seemed to be settling upon the country, and we four were beginning to hope that the time was at hand when we might safely go off with our shares of the plunder. In a moment, however, our hopes were shattered by our being arrested as the murderers of Achmet.

"It came about in this way. When the rajah put his jewels into the hands of Achmet he did it because he knew that he was a trusty man. They are suspicious folk in the East, however: so what does this rajah do but take a second even more

depose [dipóuz] v.
퇴위하다
penal [píːnəl] adj.
형벌의
penal servitude for life:
종신형
commute [kəmjúːt] v.
감형하다

trusty servant and set him to play the spy upon the first? The second man was ordered never to let Achmet out of his sight, and he followed him like his shadow. He went after him that night and saw him pass through the doorway. Of course he thought he had taken refuge in the fort, and applied for admission there himself next day, but could find no trace of Achmet. This seemed to him so strange that he spoke about it to a sergeant of guides, who brought it to the ears of the commandant. A thorough search was quickly made, and the body was discovered. Thus at the very moment that we thought that all was safe we were all four seized and brought to trial on a charge of murder—three of us because we had held the gate that night, and the fourth because he was known to have been in the company of the murdered man. Not a word about the jewels came out at the trial, for the rajah had been **deposed** and driven out of India: so no one had any particular interest in them. The murder, however, was clearly made out, and it was certain that we must all have been concerned in it. The three Sikhs got **penal servitude for life**, and I was condemned to death, though my sentence was afterwards **commuted** into the same as the others.

"It was rather a queer position that we found ourselves in then. There we were all four tied by the leg and with precious little chance of ever getting out again, while we each held a secret which might have put each of us in a palace if we could only have made use of it. It was enough to make a man eat his heart out to have to stand the kick and the cuff of every petty jack-in-office, to have rice to eat and water to drink, when that gorgeous fortune was ready for him outside, just waiting to be picked up. It might have driven me mad; but I was always a pretty stubborn one, so I just held on and bided my time.

"At last it seemed to me to have come. I was changed from Agra to Madras, and from there to Blair Island in the Andamans. There are very few white convicts at this settlement, and, as I had behaved well from the first, I soon found myself a sort of privileged person. I was given a hut in Hope Town, which is a small place on the slopes of Mount Harriet, and I was left pretty much to myself. It is a **dreary**, fever-stricken place, and all beyond our little clearings was **infested** with wild cannibal natives, who were ready enough to blow a poisoned dart at us if they saw a chance. There was digging, and ditching, and yam-planting, and a dozen other things to be done, so we were busy enough all day; though in the evening we had a little time to ourselves. Among other things, I learned to dispense drugs for the surgeon, and picked up a **smattering** of his knowledge. All the time I was on the lookout for a chance of escape; but it is hundreds of miles from any other land, and there is little or no wind in those seas: so it was a terribly difficult job to get away.

"The surgeon, Dr. Somerton, was a fast, sporting young chap, and the other young officers would meet in his rooms of an evening and play cards. The **surgery**, where I used to make up my drugs, was next to his sitting-room, with a small window

---

dreary [dríəri] adj.
우울한, 황량한
infest [infést] v.
횡행하다, 들끓다
smattering [smǽtəriŋ] n.
약간, 조금, 수박 겉핥기의 지식

surgery [sə́:rdʒəri] n.
수술실

between us. Often, if I felt lonesome, I used to turn out the lamp in the surgery, and then, standing there, I could hear their talk and watch their play. I am fond of a hand at cards myself, and it was almost as good as having one to watch the others. There was Major Sholto, Captain Morstan, and Lieutenant Bromley Brown, who were in command of the native troops, and there was the surgeon himself, and two or three prison-officials, crafty old hands who played a nice sly safe game. A very snug little party they used to make.

"Well, there was one thing which very soon struck me, and that was that the soldiers used always to lose and the civilians to win. Mind, I don't say that there was anything unfair, but so it was. These prison-chaps had done little else than play cards ever since they had been at the Andamans, and they knew each other's game to a point, while the others just played to pass the time and threw their cards down anyhow. Night after night the soldiers got up poorer men, and the poorer they got the more keen they were to play. Major Sholto was the hardest hit. He used to pay in notes and gold at first, but soon it came to notes of hand and for big sums. He sometimes would win for a few deals, just to give him heart, and then the luck would set in against him worse than ever. All day he would wander about as black as thunder, and he **took to** drinking a deal more than was good for him.

"One night he lost even more heavily than usual. I was sitting in my hut when he and Captain Morstan came stumbling along on the way to their

---

take to:
습관이 되다, 좋아하게 되다

quarters. They were bosom friends, those two, and never far apart. The major was raving about his losses.

"'It's all up, Morstan,' he was saying, as they passed my hut. 'I shall have to **send in my papers**. I am a ruined man.'

"'Nonsense, old **chap**!' said the other, slapping him upon the shoulder. 'I've had a nasty **facer** myself, but—' That was all I could hear, but it was enough to set me thinking.

"A couple of days later Major Sholto was strolling on the beach: so I took the chance of speaking to him.

"'I wish to have your advice, major,' said I.

"'Well, Small, what is it?' he asked, taking his cheroot from his lips.

"'I wanted to ask you, sir,' said I, 'who is the proper person to whom hidden treasure should be handed over. I know where half a million worth lies, and, as I cannot use it myself, I thought perhaps the best thing that I could do would be to hand it over to the proper authorities, and then perhaps they would get my sentence shortened for me.'

"'Half a million, Small?' he gasped, looking hard at me to see if I was in earnest.

"'Quite that, sir—in jewels and pearls. It lies there ready for any one. And the queer thing about it is that the real owner is outlawed and cannot hold property, so that it belongs to the first comer.'

"'To government, Small,' he stammered, 'to government.' But he said it in a halting fashion, and I knew in my heart that I had got him.

---

send in one's papers:
사직하다

chap [tʃæp] n.
사내, 친구

facer [féisər] n.
예상치 못한 타격, 손실

rash [ræʃ] adj.
무모한, 무분별한
repent [ripént] v.
후회하다, 뉘우치다, 참회하다
twitch [twitʃ] n.
경련

"'You think, then, sir, that I should give the information to the Governor-General?' said I, quietly.

"'Well, well, you must not do anything **rash**, or that you might **repent**. Let me hear all about it, Small. Give me the facts.'

"I told him the whole story, with small changes so that he could not identify the places. When I had finished he stood stock still and full of thought. I could see by the **twitch** of his lip that there was a struggle going on within him.

"'This is a very important matter, Small,' he said, at last. 'You must not say a word to any one about it, and I shall see you again soon.'

"Two nights later he and his friend Captain Morstan came to my hut in the dead of the night with a lantern.

"'I want you just to let Captain Morstan hear that story from your own lips, Small,' said he.

"I repeated it as I had told it before.

"'**It rings true**, eh?' said he. 'It's good enough to act upon?'

"Captain Morstan nodded.

"'Look here, Small,' said the major. 'We have been talking it over, my friend here and I, and we have come to the conclusion that this secret of yours is hardly a government matter, after all, but is a private concern of your own, which of course you have the power of disposing of as you think best. Now, the question is, what price would you ask for it? We might be inclined to take it up, and at least look into it, if we could agree as to terms.' He tried to speak in a cool, careless way, but his eyes were shining with excitement and greed.

it rings true:
사실로 들린다, 사실인 것 같다

"'Why, as to that, gentlemen,' I answered, trying also to be cool, but feeling as excited as he did, 'there is only one bargain which a man in my position can make. I shall want you to help me to my freedom, and to help my three companions to theirs. We shall then take you into partnership, and give you a fifth share to divide between you.'

"'Hum!' said he. 'A fifth share! That is not very tempting.'

"'It would come to fifty thousand apiece,' said I.

"'But how can we gain your freedom? You know very well that you ask an impossibility.'

"'Nothing of the sort,' I answered. 'I have thought it all out to the last detail. The only **bar** to our escape is that we can get no boat fit for the voyage, and no **provisions** to last us for so long a

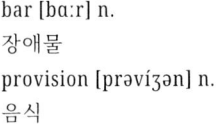

bar [bɑːr] n.
장애물
provision [prəvíʒən] n.
음식

yawl [jɔːl] n.
소형 보트

flinch [flintʃ] v.
주춤하다, 움찔하다, 물러서다

leave of absent:
휴가, 말미

time. There are plenty of little yachts and **yawls** at Calcutta or Madras which would serve our turn well. Do you bring one over. We shall engage to get aboard her by night, and if you will drop us on any part of the Indian coast you will have done your part of the bargain.'

"'If there were only one,' he said.

"'None or all,' I answered. 'We have sworn it. The four of us must always act together.'

"'You see, Morstan,' said he, 'Small is a man of his word. He does not **flinch** from his friend. I think we may very well trust him.'

"'It's a dirty business,' the other answered. 'Yet, as you say, the money will save our commissions handsomely.'

"'Well, Small,' said the major, 'we must, I suppose, try and meet you. We must first, of course, test the truth of your story. Tell me where the box is hid, and I shall get **leave of absence** and go back to India in the monthly relief-boat to inquire into the affair.'

"'Not so fast,' said I, growing colder as he got hot. 'I must have the consent of my three comrades. I tell you that it is four or none with us.'

"'Nonsense!' he broke in. 'What have three black fellows to do with our agreement?'

"'Black or blue,' said I, 'they are in with me, and we all go together.'

"Well, the matter ended by a second meeting, at which Mahomet Singh, Abdullah Khan, and Dost Akbar were all present. We talked the matter over again, and at last we came to an arrangement. We were to provide both the officers with charts of the part of the Agra fort and mark the place in the wall where the treasure was hid. Major Sholto was to go to India to test our story. If he found the box he was to leave it there, to send out a small yacht provisioned for a voyage, which was to lie off Rutland Island, and to which we were to make our way, and finally to return to his duties. Captain Morstan was then to apply for leave of absence, to meet us at Agra, and there we were to have a final division of the treasure, he taking the major's share as well as his own. All this we sealed by the most solemn oaths that the mind could think or the lips utter. I sat up all night with paper and ink, and by the morning I had the two charts all ready, signed with the sign of four,—that is, of Abdullah, Akbar, Mahomet, and myself.

"Well, gentlemen, I **weary** you with my long story, and I know that my friend Mr. Jones is impatient to get me safely stowed in **chokey**. I'll make it as short as I can. The **villain** Sholto went off to India, but he never came back again. Captain Morstan showed me his name among a list of passengers in one of the mail-boats very shortly afterwards. His uncle had died, leaving him a fortune, and he had left the army, yet he could stoop to treat five men as he had treated us. Morstan went over to Agra shortly afterwards, and found, as we expected, that the treasure was indeed gone. The **scoundrel** had stolen it all, without carrying out one of the conditions on which we had sold him the secret. From that day I lived only for vengeance. I thought of it by day and I **nursed** it by night. It became an overpowering, absorbing

---

weary [wíəri] v.
피곤하게 하다, 진력(싫증)나게 하다
choky, chokey [tʃóuki] n.
감옥
villain [vílən] n.
악한, 악당
scoundrel [skáundrəl] n.
무뢰한, 악당
nurse [nəːrs] v.
(마음에) 품다, 키우다

passion with me. I cared nothing for the law,—nothing for the gallows. To escape, to track down Sholto, to have my hand upon his throat,—that was my one thought. Even the Agra treasure had come to be a smaller thing in my mind than the slaying of Sholto.

"Well, I have set my mind on many things in this life, and never one which I did not carry out. But it was weary years before my time came. I have told you that I had picked up something of medicine. One day when Dr. Somerton was down with a fever a little Andaman Islander was picked up by a convict-gang in the woods. He was sick to death, and had gone to a lonely place to die. I took him in hand, though he was as **venomous** as a young snake, and after a couple of months I got him all right and able to walk. He took a kind of fancy to me then, and would hardly go back to his woods, but was always hanging about my hut. I learned a little of his **lingo** from him, and this made him all the fonder of me.

"Tonga—for that was his name—was a fine boatman, and owned a big, roomy canoe of his own. When I found that he was devoted to me and would do anything to serve me, I saw my chance of escape. I talked it over with him. He was to bring his boat round on a certain night to an old wharf which was never guarded, and there he was to pick me up. I gave him directions to have several gourds of water and a lot of yams, cocoa-nuts, and sweet potatoes.

"He was **stanch** and true, was little Tonga. No man ever had a more faithful mate. At the night

---

venomous [vénəməs] adj.
악의 가득한, 독성의
lingo [líŋgou] n.
지방어, 사투리, 특정 언어

stanch, staunch [stɑːntʃ, stɔːntʃ] adj.
충실한, 확고한

named he had his boat at the wharf. As it chanced, however, there was one of the convict-guard down there,—a vile Pathan who had never missed a chance of insulting and injuring me. I had always vowed vengeance, and now I had my chance. It was as if fate had placed him in my way that I might pay my debt before I left the island. He stood on the bank with his back to me, and his carbine on his shoulder. I looked about for a stone to beat out his brains with, but none could I see.

"Then a queer thought came into my head and showed me where I could lay my hand on a weapon. I sat down in the darkness and unstrapped my wooden leg. With three long hops I was on him. He put his carbine to his shoulder, but I struck him full, and knocked the whole front of his skull in. You can see the split in the wood now where I hit him. We both went down together, for I could not keep my balance, but when I got up I found him still lying quiet enough. I made for the boat, and in an hour we were well out at sea. Tonga had brought all his earthly possessions with him, his arms and his gods. Among other things, he had a long bamboo spear, and some Andaman cocoa-nut matting, with which I made a sort of sail. For ten days we were beating about, trusting to luck, and on the eleventh we were picked up by a trader which was going from Singapore to Jiddah with a cargo of Malay pilgrims. They were a **rum** crowd, and Tonga and I soon managed to settle down among them. They had one very good quality: they let you alone and asked no questions.

"Well, if I were to tell you all the adventures

---

rum [rʌm] adj.
기묘한, 이상한

chum [tʃʌm] n.
친구

bethink [biθíŋk] v.
생각하다, 상기하다

that my little **chum** and I went through, you would not thank me, for I would have you here until the sun was shining. Here and there we drifted about the world, something always turning up to keep us from London. All the time, however, I never lost sight of my purpose. I would dream of Sholto at night. A hundred times I have killed him in my sleep. At last, however, some three or four years ago, we found ourselves in England. I had no great difficulty in finding where Sholto lived, and I set to work to discover whether he had realized the treasure, or if he still had it. I made friends with someone who could help me,—I name no names, for I don't want to get any one else in a hole,—and I soon found that he still had the jewels. Then I tried to get at him in many ways; but he was pretty sly, and had always two prize-fighters, besides his sons and his khitmutgar, on guard over him.

"One day, however, I got word that he was dying. I hurried at once to the garden, mad that he should slip out of my clutches like that, and, looking through the window, I saw him lying in his bed, with his sons on each side of him. I'd have come through and taken my chance with the three of them, only even as I looked at him his jaw dropped, and I knew that he was gone. I got into his room that same night, though, and I searched his papers to see if there was any record of where he had hidden our jewels. There was not a line, however: so I came away, bitter and savage as a man could be. Before I left I **bethought** me that if I ever met my Sikh friends again it would be a satisfaction to know that I had left some mark of our hatred: so I scrawled down the sign of the four of us, as it had been on the chart, and I pinned it on his bosom. It was too much that he should be taken to the grave without some token from the men whom he had robbed and befooled.

"We earned a living at this time by my exhibiting poor Tonga at fairs and other such places as the black cannibal. He would eat raw meat and dance his war-dance: so we always had a hatful of pennies after a day's work. I still heard all the news from Pondicherry Lodge, and for some years there was no news to hear, except that they were hunting for the treasure. At last, however, came what we had waited for so long. The treasure had been found. It was up at the top of the house, in Mr. Bartholomew Sholto's chemical laboratory. I came at once and had a look at the place, but I could not see how with my wooden leg I was to make my way up to it. I learned, however, about a trap-door in the roof, and also about Mr. Sholto's supper-hour. It seemed to me that I could manage the thing easily through Tonga. I brought him out with me with a long rope wound round his waist. He could climb like a cat, and he soon made his way through the roof, but, as ill luck would have it, Bartholomew Sholto was still in the room, to his cost. Tonga thought he had done something very clever in killing him, for when I came up by the rope I found him **strutting** about as proud as a peacock. Very much surprised was he when I made at him with the rope's end and cursed him for a little blood-thirsty imp. I took the treasure-box and let it down, and then slid down myself,

strut [strʌt] v.
뽐내며 걷다

having first left the sign of the four upon the table, to show that the jewels had come back at last to those who had most right to them. Tonga then pulled up the rope, closed the window, and made off the way that he had come.

"I don't know that I have anything else to tell you. I had heard a **waterman** speak of the speed of Smith's launch, the *Aurora*, so I thought she would be a handy craft for our escape. I engaged with old Smith, and was to give him a big sum if he got us safe to our ship. He knew, no doubt, that there was some screw loose, but he was not in our secrets. All this is the truth, and if I tell it to you, gentlemen, it is not to amuse you,—for you have not done me a very good turn,—but it is because I believe the best defence I can make is just to hold back nothing, but let all the world know how badly I have myself been served by Major Sholto, and how innocent I am of the death of his son."

"A very remarkable **account**," said Sherlock Holmes. "A fitting **wind-up** to an extremely interesting case. There is nothing at all new to me in the latter part of your narrative, except that you brought your own rope. That I did not know. By the way, I had hoped that Tonga had lost all his darts; yet he managed to shoot one at us in the boat."

"He had lost them all, sir, except the one which was in his blow-pipe at the time."

"Ah, of course," said Holmes. "I had not thought of that."

"Is there any other point which you would like to ask about?" asked the convict, affably.

connoisseur [kànəsə́ːr, -súər / kɔ̀n-] n.
감정가, 감식가
under lock and key:
자물쇠를 채워, 투옥되어
obliged [əbláidʒd] adj.
감사한, 고마운

wary [wéəri] adj.
경계하는, 조심하는

"I think not, thank you," my companion answered.

"Well, Holmes," said Athelney Jones, "You are a man to be humored, and we all know that you are a **connoisseur** of crime, but duty is duty, and I have gone rather far in doing what you and your friend asked me. I shall feel more at ease when we have our story-teller here safe **under lock and key**. The cab still waits, and there are two inspectors down-stairs. I am much **obliged** to you both for your assistance. Of course you will be wanted at the trial. Good-night to you."

"Good-night, gentlemen both," said Jonathan Small.

"You first, Small," remarked the **wary** Jones as they left the room. "I'll take particular care that you don't club me with your wooden leg, whatever you

may have done to the gentleman at the Andaman Isles."

"Well, and there is the end of our little drama," I remarked, after we had set some time smoking in silence. "I fear that it may be the last investigation in which I shall have the chance of studying your methods. Miss Morstan has done me the honor to accept me as a husband in prospective."

He gave a most dismal groan.

"I feared as much," said he. "I really cannot congratulate you."

I was a little hurt.

"Have you any reason to be dissatisfied with my choice?" I asked.

"Not at all. I think she is one of the most charming young ladies I ever met, and might have been most useful in such work as we have been doing. She had a decided genius that way: witness the way in which she preserved that Agra plan from all the other papers of her father. But love is an emotional thing, and whatever is emotional is opposed to that true cold reason which I place above all things. I should never marry myself, lest I bias my judgment."

"I trust," said I, laughing, "that my judgment may survive the **ordeal**. But you look weary."

"Yes, the reaction is already upon me. I shall be as **limp** as a **rag** for a week."

"Strange," said I, "how terms of what in another man I should call laziness alternate with your fits of splendid energy and vigor."

"Yes," he answered, "there are in me the makings of a very fine loafer and also of a pretty spry sort of fellow. I often think of those lines of old Goethe,—

**Schade dass** die Natur nur *einen* Mensch aus dir schuf, Denn zum würdigen Mann war und zum Schelmen der Stoff.

"By the way, **apropos** of this Norwood business, you see that they had, as I surmised, a **confederate** in the house, who could be none other than Lal Rao, the butler: so Jones actually has the undivided honor of having caught one fish in his great haul."

"The division seems rather unfair," I remarked. "You have done all the work in this business. I get a wife out of it, Jones gets the credit, pray what remains for you?"

"For me," said Sherlock Holmes, "there still remains the cocaine-bottle." And he stretched his long white hand up for it.

---

Schade dass ~:
"선인과 악인을 만들 수 있음에도, 자연은 오직 그대, 하나의 존재만을 만드는구나."

apropos of~ [æ̀prəpóu]
~에 관하여

confederate [kənfédərit] n.
공범

# 네 사람의 서명 시놉시스

## 1. 추리의 과학

   홈즈는 마약을 복용하는 습관이 있는데, 정신을 맑게 하고 기분을 돋운다고 생각하기 때문이다. 왓슨이 그의 중독성 탐닉을 비판하며, 그의 뇌에 안 좋은 영향을 미친다고 말한다. 왓슨이 홈즈의 정신만이 아니라 몸에도 미칠 돌이킬 수 없는 손상을 우려한다.
   홈즈가 인위적인 자극제가 아닌 정신적인 고양高揚을 갈구한다고 왓슨에게 말한다.
   홈즈가 왓슨이 아침에 어딜 갔다 왔는지 추리하여 그의 추리 능력을 보이고, 관찰과 추리의 차이점을 논증한다.
   홈즈의 추리 과학에 흥미를 느낀 왓슨이 보다 어려운 문제를 제시한다. 홈즈에게 시계를 하나 건네고는, 그 시계의 원래 주인의 성격이나 버릇 등에 관해 묻는다. 홈즈가 너무나 정확히 추리하여 왓슨을 화나게 하는데, 자신의 불행한 형의 문제를 두고 그를 속였다고 생각하기 때문이다. 홈즈가 추론 과정을 설명하고, 왓슨은 홈즈의 독특한 재능을 인정하게 된다.
   홈즈가 너무나 황량하고 우울하며 공허한 세상에 관해 얘기하고, 본인의 능력을 펼칠 기회가 없음을 한탄한다.
   홈즈의 불만에 응답이라도 하듯이, 메리 모스턴이라는 젊은 여성이 그의 조언을 얻기 위해 찾아온다.

## 2. 사건 진술

방안에 들어서며 모스턴 양이 심한 불안함을 보인다.
모스턴이 자기의 사건을 이야기한다.

모스턴의 아버지는 인도의 한 연대에 배속되어 있었으며, 안다만 제도에서 죄수들을 관리하는 장교로 근무했다.
1878년 12월, 아버지로부터 전보가 왔는데, 런던에 무사히 도착했으며, 랭험 호텔로 오라는 내용이었다. 모스턴이 호텔에 도착해보니, 아버지가 간밤에 외출하여 아직 돌아오지 않았음을 알게 되었다. 그녀가 온종일 기다려봤지만, 그는 돌아오지 않았다. 아버지를 찾으려 이런저런 노력을 해봤으나, 여태까지 감감무소식이다.
모스턴이 아버지의 유일한 친구인 숄토 소령과 연락을 하지만, 소령은 자신의 동료가 영국에 왔다는 사실도 모르고 있었다.
6년 전, 한 신문에서 모스턴의 주소를 알려달라는 광고를 보게 되었다. 그녀의 고용인인 세실 포레스터 부인의 조언에 따라 그 광고에 답장을 보냈다. 그 이후로 어느 익명의 자선가로부터 매년 귀중한 진주가 오기 시작했다.
그러다가 오늘 아침, 정체불명의 사람으로부터 편지를 받게 되었는데, 그녀가 부당한 대우를 받고 있으며, 밤 7시에 라이시엄 극장에서 만나자는 내용이었다.

홈즈가 왓슨과 모스턴에게 이 미지의 인물을 만나러 같이 가자고 제안한다. 6시에 만날 약속을 하고 모스턴이 떠나고, 왓슨이 홈즈에게 그녀가 아주 매력적임을 얘기한다.
홈즈가 조사를 하기 위해 방을 나선다.
왓슨은 모스턴에게 호감을 갖기에는 그의 장래가 너무도 암담함을 깨닫는다. 왓슨은 남자답게 있는 그대로의 현실을 받아들이기로 결심한다.

## 3. 해결책을 찾아서

　홈즈가 조사를 마치고 돌아와, 왓슨에게 숄토 소령의 부고 기사를 신문에서 찾아봤다고 말한다. 그는 숄토의 죽음과 모스턴이 받은 진주 사이에 연관성이 있다고 생각한다.
　모스턴이 와서 아버지의 책상에서 찾은 흥미로운 종이를 홈즈에게 보여준다. 종이에는 커다란 건물의 약도가 그려져 있으며, 그 건물 그림 옆으로 다음과 같은 글이 적혀 있다.
　"네 사람의 서명 - 조너선 스몰, 마호메트 싱, 압둘라 칸, 도스트 악바르."
　그들이 라이시엄 극장에 도착해보니, 한 마부가 다가와 그들의 신원을 확인한다. 마부가 그들에게 승차해 달라고 부탁하고는, 일행을 태우고 빠른 속도로 안개 낀 거리를 질주한다.
　알 수 없는 목적지로 향하는 도중에, 왓슨이 아프가니스탄에서 겪은 모험담을 이야기하여 모스턴을 안심시키고 즐겁게 하려고 한다.
　일행이 심상치 않은 분위기의 동네에 있는 어느 집 앞에 도착하며, 한 힌두 하인에 의해 집안으로 안내된다.


## 4. 대머리 사내의 이야기

　그들이 작고한 숄토 소령의 아들인 새디어스 숄토라는 인물과 만난다.
　새디어스 숄토는 무심결에 모스턴 아버지의 사망을 언급하는데, 왓슨이 이러한 슬픈 소식을 아무렇지도 않게 말하는 숄토의 무신경함에 분노한다.
　숄토가 모스턴이 정당한 보상을 받게 하겠다고 약속하고, 폰디체리 저택에 사는 그의 쌍둥이 형인 바솔로뮤와 이와 관련하여 논쟁을 벌인 사실을 얘기한다.
　숄토가 막대한 부를 가지고 인도에서 은퇴했던 그의 아버지 숄토 소령에 관해 얘기한다.

숄토 소령은 모종의 위협을 받는 듯이 보였으며, 나무 의족을 한 사람을 극도로 두려워했다. 한번은 어느 의족을 한 사람을 권총으로 쏜 적도 있는데, 그 사람은 무고한 상인에 불과했다.

1882년 초에 숄토 소령은 인도에서 편지를 하나 받게 되는데, 그 편지에 엄청난 충격을 받고는 몸져누워 생을 마치게 되었다. 임종 순간에, 소령은 그의 친구 모스턴 대위와 그의 딸 메리 모스턴에게 잘못을 저질렀다고 두 아들에게 고백하는데, 자신과 모스턴 대위가 인도에서 얻은 아그라 보물을 혼자 독차지하려는 탐욕으로 말미암았다고 말한다.

모스턴 대위가 군 복무를 마치고 런던으로 돌아왔을 때, 숄토와 보물 문제로 논쟁을 벌였는데, 이때 비극적인 사고에 의한 죽음을 맞게 되었다.

숄토 소령이 보물을 모스턴 대위의 딸과 나눠 가지라는 마지막 유언을 남겼다.

그가 보물의 행방을 말하려는 찰나, 창가에 있는 어느 낯선 남자를 발견하고 공포에 질리게 되는데, 그 사나이는 강렬한 악의의 표정으로 방안을 보고 있었다. 숄토 형제가 창으로 달려가 봤으나, 침입자는 사라지고 없었다. 형제가 다시 침대로 돌아왔을 때는 아버지가 이미 세상을 떠난 후였다.

이튿날 아침, 형제는 아버지의 방을 어지러이 뒤진 흔적과, 아버지의 가슴에 놓인 한 장의 종이를 발견하는데, 종이에는 "네 사람의 서명"이라는 글이 적혀 있었다.

새디어스 숄토는 그의 형 바솔로뮤를 설득하여 모스턴의 주소를 찾아냈고, 아버지의 유언대로 모스턴에게 매년 진주를 보냈다.

새디어스 숄토는 어제 모스턴에게 연락을 하게 되는데, 바솔로뮤가 보물을 찾았기 때문으로, 그와 모스턴이 바솔로뮤에게 가서 그녀의 정당한 몫을 요구해야 한다고 생각했다.


보물의 가치는 막대할 것으로 추정되며, 모스턴은 영국에서 가장 부유한 상속인이 될 것으로 예상된다. 모스턴을 축하해 주는 게 당연하지만, 왓슨의 마음은 납처럼 무겁다.

## 5. 폰디체리 저택의 비극

일행이 어둠과 적막함으로 둘러싸인 폰디체리 저택에 도착한다. 집에 들어가기 전에 문지기와 논쟁을 한다.

새디어스 숄토가 저택 안으로 들어가고, 그의 쌍둥이 형 바솔로뮤에게 무언가 심상치 않은 일이 벌어졌음을 느끼고 겁에 질린다.

홈즈와 왓슨이 바솔로뮤가 안으로 문을 잠근 채 방에 있으며, 하인의 부름에도 아무 대답을 하지 않고 있음을 알게 된다. 홈즈가 열쇠 구멍을 통해 무언가 사악한 일이 벌어졌음을 감지한다.

홈즈와 왓슨이 문을 부수고 들어가 보니, 바솔로뮤가 기이한 미소를 짓고 사망해 있는 걸 발견한다. 옆 테이블에 놓인 종이엔 "네 사람의 서명"이란 문구가 적혀 있다. 독화살이 그의 귀 바로 위에 박혀 있으며, 아그라 보물은 사라지고 없다.

## 6. 셜록 홈즈가 현장을 조사하다

셜록 홈즈가 의족 자국을 발견하는데, 의족을 한 사내가 로프를 이용하여 창문을 통해 침입했음을 나타낸다. 홈즈가 의족을 한 사내의 침입을 도와준 공범이 있으며, 그 공범은 천장에 난 구멍을 통해 들어왔다고 추론한다.

그들이 천장에 난 구멍을 통해 다락방으로 오르는데, 범인이 침입한 경로로 추정되는 지붕으로 통하는 들창이 있다. 바닥에 작은 맨발 자국이 발견되어 왓슨을 놀라게 하는데, 어린아이가 이 사악한 범죄에 연루되었다고 생각하기 때문이다.

홈즈가 공범이 크레오소트를 밟았음을 알게 되고, 크레오소트의 강한 냄새를 이용하여 범인을 잡을 수 있다고 생각한다.

셜록 홈즈가 방에 들어서는 런던 경찰청 형사 애셜니 존스를 맞는다.

애셜니 존스가 몇몇 조사를 하고, 새디어스 숄토를 의심하는데, 그가 피해자를 마지막으로 본 사람이기 때문이다. 숄토가 애셜니 존스에 의해 체포될 때, 홈즈가 그의 억울한 혐의를 벗겨주겠다고 약속한다.

홈즈가 두 명의 범죄자가 사건에 연루되어 있으며, 그중 한 명은 조너선 스몰이라는 인물로 나무로 된 의족을 하고 있으며, 과거에 죄수였다고 애셜니 존스에게 말한다.

홈즈가 왓슨에게 메리 모스턴을 집으로 바래다주고, 토비라는 개를 셔먼이라는 사람한테서 빌려와달라고 부탁한다.


## 7. 통 이야기

왓슨이 모스턴을 집에 데려다주고, 셔먼의 집을 찾는다.

왓슨이 문을 노크하지만, 그를 못된 장난꾼으로 오해한 셔먼이 험한 말을 하며 위협하여 내쫓으려 한다. 왓슨이 셜록 홈즈를 언급하자, 셔먼이 곧바로 그를 반가이 맞이한다.

왓슨이 토비를 끌고 폰디체리 저택으로 돌아온다.

홈즈가 목에 랜턴을 매고 지붕에서 범인의 흔적을 조사한다. 홈즈가 지붕에서 땅으로 내려오고, 독화살이 담긴 작은 주머니를 왓슨에게 보여주는데, 범인이 서두르는 와중에 떨어뜨린 것이다.

홈즈가 토비에게 크레오소트에 적신 손수건을 냄새 맡게 하고, 그 냄새를 쫓게 한다. 냄새를 추적하는 토비를 따라가는 와중에 날이 밝는다.

홈즈가 왓슨에게 모스턴 대위의 도면에 적힌 이름 중 하나인 조너선 스몰이 의족을 한 사내라는 결론에 도달한 이유를 설명한다. 홈즈는 인도에서 죄수를 관리하던 장교였던 모스턴 대위와 숄토 소령이 숨겨진 보물에 대해 알게 되었고, 조너선 스몰이 그들에게 도면을 그려줬다고 추측한다. 도면을 통해 장교들 또는 둘 중 하나가 보물을 찾아 영국으로 왔으나, 스몰과의 약속을 저버렸다. 홈즈는 또한 스몰이 인도에서 탈출했으며, 숄토 소령의 마지막 순간에 창문에 나타났던 낯선 인물이 바로 스몰일 것으로 추정한다. 홈즈의 주장에 따르면, 스몰이 바솔로뮤가 다락방의 보물을 발견했다는 사실을 알게 되었고, 그의 공범의 도움을 받아 방에 침입했다. 홈즈는 바솔로뮤 사망의 책임이 스몰의 공범에게 있다고 생각한다.

토비가 한 곳에서 머뭇머뭇하며 어슬렁거려 홈즈를 안달 나게 한다.

토비가 다시 달려가기 시작하는데, 크레오소트로 범벅이 된 통 앞에 이르게 된다. 잘못된 길로 왔음을 알게 된 홈즈와 왓슨이 웃음을 터트린다.

## 8. 베이커 거리 수사대

　홈즈와 왓슨이 개가 망설였던 장소로 다시 돌아가는데, 거기서 냄새의 흔적이 엇갈린 것으로 보이기 때문이다. 토비가 다른 방향으로 뛰어서 이번에는 부둣가로 인도하며, 범인들이 배를 타고 도망갔음을 짐작하게 한다.
　홈즈와 왓슨이 모드케이 스미스라는 사람의 작은 벽돌집 앞에 이르게 된다. 스미스 부인을 만나는데, 그녀의 남편은 증기선 오로라를 타고 나가 아직 돌아오지 않았다. 그녀가 남편이 의족을 한 사내와 같이 갔다고 말한다.
　집으로 돌아오는 길에, 홈즈가 베이커 거리 수사대 중의 하나인 위긴스에게 전보를 친다.
　거리의 아이들이 집에 오자, 홈즈가 그들에게 증기선 오로라를 찾으라고 하고, 새로운 사실을 발견하면 즉시 알려달라고 지시한다.
　아이들이 간 후에, 홈즈가 조너선 스몰의 공범을 언급하는데, 사건 현장의 증거로부터 야만인으로 추정한다. 홈즈가 지명사전을 참고하여, 스몰의 공범이 안다만 제도의 원주민으로 난쟁이 같이 작은 체구에 흉측한 외모를 가졌을 것으로 생각한다.

## 9. 끊어진 고리

　왓슨이 세실 포레스터 부인과 모스턴을 방문하여, 그동안 벌어진 일들을 설명하고 집으로 돌아온다.
　홈즈가 왓슨에게 막다른 벽에 부딪혔다고 말하는데, 위긴스와 그 밖의 다른 어떤 경로를 통해서도 아무런 단서를 얻지 못했기 때문이다.
　이른 새벽 왓슨이 깨어나 보니, 홈즈가 허름한 선원 복장을 하고 있다. 홈즈가 왓슨에게 마지막 시도로 템스강으로 가 보려 한다고 말하고는 방을 나선다.
　오후 3시에 애셜니 존스가 왓슨을 찾아오는데, 홈즈로부터 집으로 오라는 연락을 받았기 때문이다.

애셜니 존스가 새디어스 숄토의 알리바이가 입증되어 그를 석방했다고 말한다. 존스는 그의 직업적인 신망이 위태로워졌다고 걱정한다.

이때, 어느 괴팍한 노인이 방으로 와서 셜록 홈즈를 찾는다. 그는 모데카이 스미스의 배가 어디 있는지 알고 있으나, 셜록 홈즈에게만 얘기할 수 있다고 말한다.

이후에, 그 노인은 왓슨과 애셜니 존스에게 장난을 친 셜록 홈즈로 밝혀진다. 홈즈는 노인으로 변장을 하여 수사를 했던 것이다.

홈즈가 애셜니 존스에게 두 범인의 체포를 장담하고, 7시에 웨스트민스터 선착장에 빠른 속도의 증기선을 대기시켜 달라고 말한다. 또한 범인들로부터 보물을 찾게 되면 왓슨이 메리 모스턴에게 보물을 전달하게 해 달라고 형사에게 요청한다.

## 10. 원주민의 최후

저녁 식사 후, 일행은 웨스트민스터 선착장에 도착한다. 홈즈가 애셜니 존스에게 얘기한 증기선이 대기하고 있다.

그들이 증기선에 승선한다. 홈즈가 애셜니 존스에게 런던탑 쪽으로 가서 제이컵슨 조선소 맞은편에 대라고 말한다.

홈즈가 그가 조녀선 스몰이라면 어떻게 오로라 증기선을 숨길지를 생각했다고 말한다. 스몰이라면 배의 조그마한 결함을 고친다는 핑계로 조선소에 숨겼을 거로 생각하고, 선원 복장을 하고는 강을 따라 모든 조선소를 뒤졌으며, 오로라가 의족을 한 사내에 의해 제이컵슨 조선소에 맡겨진 걸 알게 되었다.

조선소의 입구를 감시하는 중에, 오로라 증기선이 나타나 빠른 속도로 항해하기 시작한다. 홈즈가 기관사에게 전속력으로 추격하라고 지시한다.

추격하는 배와의 거리가 가까워지자, 애셜니 존스가 그들에게 멈추라고 소리 지른다. 왓슨은 오로라의 고물에서 어느 의족을 한 사내가 주먹을 휘두르며 갈라진 고음의 욕설을 퍼붓는 것을 목격한다.

이때 한 작은 체구의 사내가 갑자기 모습을 드러내는데, 홈즈와 왓슨이 위험이 닥쳐옴을 감지하고 권총을 꺼내 든다. 이 조그만 야만인이 독침이 든 바람총을 꺼내어 불려는 순간, 홈즈와 왓슨이 권총을 발사한다. 야만인이 총에 맞고 배 밖으로 추락하여 강물 속으로 사라진다.

조너선 스몰이 갯벌에서 잡히고, 아그라 보물이 오로라의 갑판 위에서 발견된다.

홈즈와 왓슨이 야만인의 흉악한 독침을 간신히 피했음을 나중에 알게 된다.

## 11. 아그라의 보물

그들이 사로잡은 범인과 보물 상자를 선실로 옮긴다.

조너선 스몰이 어떻게 바솔로뮤가 난쟁이 야만인인 통가에 의해 죽었는지를 말하고, 그 저주받은 아그라 보물로 인해 그 보물을 차지한 사람들이 불행에 빠지게 됐는지 얘기한다.

왓슨이 보물을 모스턴에게 가져다주고, 보물의 반을 갖게 된 그녀를 축하한다. 왓슨이 그동안 있었던 일을 간략히 모스턴에게 얘기한다.

스몰이 열쇠를 템스강에 버렸으므로, 왓슨이 부지깽이를 이용하여 보물 상자를 강제로 연다. 놀랍게도 상자는 텅 비어있다.

양심에 꺼려지기는 하지만, 왓슨은 안심되고 고마움을 느끼는데, 그와 모스턴의 사이에 있던 황금 장벽이 사라졌기 때문이다. 왓슨이 그의 사랑을 고백하고, 그날 밤 하나의 보물은 잃었지만 다른 하나의 보물을 얻었음을 알게 된다.

## 12. 조너선 스몰의 기이한 이야기

왓슨이 베이커 거리의 집으로 와서, 애셜니 존스에게 빈 상자를 보여준다. 스몰이 보물을 템스강에 버린 것인데, 숄토나 모스턴의 가족들이 자신의 보물을 차지하는 걸 용납할 수 없기 때문이었다.

조너선 스몰이 그의 과거를 들려준다.

스몰은 18살 무렵에 한 여자와 문제를 일으켜서, 마침 인도로 떠날 예정인 군대에 입대하게 되었다.

어느 날, 스몰은 어리석게도 갠지스강에서 수영을 했는데, 악어의 공격을 받아 오른쪽 다리를 잃었다. 같은 부대 하사인 존 홀더가 기절한 그를 구해 나왔다. 그는 상처를 치유하고 의족을 차야 했으며, 의병제대를 하게 되었다.

스몰이 에이블 화이트라는 사람의 농장에서 감독관으로 일하게 되었다. 세포이 항쟁이 일어났을 때, 그는 아그라 성채로 피신해야 했다.

스몰이 야간의 특정 시간에 마호메트 싱과 압둘라 칸이라는 두 명의 시크 군인과 어느 작은 문을 지키는 임무를 맡게 되었다.

야간 감시 업무를 시작한 3일째 되는 날 새벽 2시에, 두 명의 시크 군인이 스몰을 덮치더니 조용히 하라고 위협했다. 압둘라 칸이 스몰에게 그들과 같이 일을 도모하거나 아니면 목숨을 잃거나 둘 중 하나를 선택하라고 강요했다. 스몰은 북부 지방의 어느 군주의 보물을 차지하기 위한 그들의 계획에 동참하라는 요구를 받는데, 그 군주의 신임을 받는 하인이 그날 밤 아그라 성채로 보물을 가져올 예정이었다. 그 하인은 아흐메트라는 이름의 상인으로 위장하여, 그들의 또 다른 공모자인 도스트 악바르와 함께 오고 있었다.

스몰은 그들의 제의를 수락했으며, 네 명의 범죄자들은 아흐메트를 없애고 보물을 차지했고, 보물은 건물의 한 구석에 숨겨 놓았다.

그러나 그들의 범죄는 곧 발각되었고, 그들의 끔찍한 범죄로 인해 수감되었다. 그들은 종신형을 선고받고, 안다만 제도에서 죄수 생활을 하게 되었다.

스몰은 거기서 숄토 소령과 모스턴 대위를 만나게 됐고, 그들에게 거래를 제안했다. 보물의 5분의 1을 주는 대신에, 그와 다른 세 명의 범죄자들을 자유롭게 풀어달라는 거였다. 거래가 성사되어 보물이 숨겨진 인도로 숄토 소령을 보내기로 했다. 그러나 숄토 소령은 보물을 혼자 독차지함으로써 스몰과 다른 사람들을 배신했으며, 다시 돌아오지 않았다.

스몰은 숄토의 이 악랄한 배신에 대한 복수를 맹세했다.

한번은 스몰이 병에 걸린 통가라는 안다만 원주민을 구해 준 일이 있다. 통가의 도움으로 스몰은 감옥을 탈출하고 런던에 도착했다.

스몰이 감옥을 탈출한 소식이 숄토 소령에게 전해졌으며, 그의 생명을 재촉하는 병으로 이어졌다.

　어느 날 숄토가 죽어간다는 얘기를 들은 스몰이 폰디체리 저택으로 침입했다. 스몰은 숄토 소령의 방 창가에서 그의 마지막을 목격했으나, 숄토가 어디에 보물을 숨겼는지는 알 수가 없었다. 그가 할 수 있는 일이라고는 네 명의 이름을 암시하는 쪽지를 남기는 것뿐이었다.

　몇 년이 지나, 스몰이 바솔로뮤가 보물을 찾았다는 소식을 듣게 되었다.

　그날 밤 스몰이 통가의 도움을 받아 바솔로뮤의 방으로 침입했다. 그는 바솔로뮤가 방에 없을 것으로 생각했다. 불행히도 바솔로뮤는 통가가 지붕의 들창을 통해 방으로 들어왔을 때 아직 방 안에 있었고, 야만인의 독침에 의해 죽게 되었다.

　스몰과 통가는 스미스의 증기선 오로라를 타고 영국을 탈출하려고 하였다. 그러나 그들의 계획은 셜록 홈즈에 의해 좌절되었다.

　애셜니 존스 형사가 스몰을 체포해 간 후, 왓슨은 모스턴과 결혼하려는 자신의 결심을 얘기한다.

　사건이 종결됨에 따라, 홈즈는 다시 지치고 나른한 상태가 되는데, 그의 활력과 기운의 반작용이 시작된 탓이다.